ARTS
for Retail

Using Technology to Turn Your Consumers
into Customers and Make a Profit

RICHARD HALTER

iUniverse®

ARTS FOR RETAIL
USING TECHNOLOGY TO TURN YOUR CONSUMERS
INTO CUSTOMERS AND MAKE A PROFIT

iUniverse books may be ordered through booksellers or by contacting:

iUniverse
1663 Liberty Drive
Bloomington, IN 47403
www.iuniverse.com
1-800-Authors (1-800-288-4677)

ISBN: 978-1-4917-1552-9 (sc)
ISBN: 978-1-4917-1554-3 (hc)
ISBN: 978-1-4917-1553-6 (e)

Library of Congress Control Number: 2013921659

Printed in the United States of America.

iUniverse rev. date: 10/02/2014

This book is dedicated to the thousands of incredible individuals involved in creating these standards. If anyone is able to teach an old dog new tricks, this group can.

I like to say I've been in college since 1999, and these people are my instructors.

CONTENTS

INTRODUCTION

This is not a book about all of retailing, but rather it is about ARTS®
(Association of Retail Technology Standards) support for retailing. I got
started with ARTS to help create a way to easily interoperate between
applications. I'm not a writer, I'm an engineer. But I thought this story
needed telling.

In 1997, my company had an ASP (application service provider)
model where we collected POS (point of sale) information in XML
(Extensible Markup Language) and provided insight to the store
operator about how his or her store was doing. In doing this, we had to
interface with a wide variety of POS systems. Each had its own interface
model. We had to reverse engineer many of these systems in order to
find the content so we could populate our guidance. This made us
intimately aware of the value of a standard interface.

My supervisor, Tim Henriksen, read the announcement about
ARTS creating a group to standardize the interfaces we had been
struggling to decipher. Tim went to the CEO, Jim Melvin, and the two
of them decided that we needed to be a part of this. They chose me to
be their representative. That led me to ARTS where I met a gentleman
named Richard Mader. Mr. Mader was the executive director of ARTS.
He helped create it and then ran it until his retirement in 2012. His
leadership turned ARTS into an organization with worldwide impact.

When I started working in retail, I thought it would be relatively
simple. After all, retail is all about exchanging goods and services for
money. I give you a shirt, and you give me money—sounds trivial. Boy,
was I wrong. Each area of retail is a discipline unto itself.

Companies send their smartest people to ARTS meetings. They want to present the most positive image of their company they can muster to competitors and customers. Over the years, I've met thousands of individuals who have helped create these standards. That comment holds true for every one of them. All of them are incredible and have in-depth knowledge of their disciplines.

After reading this book, you will not be an expert in any particular discipline. However, you will become an expert on what ARTS provides for retail.

For every ARTS standard, ARTS has a vast quantity of supporting documentation. For example, one of the most adopted XML standards, POSLog, has use cases to describe things like how to sell a shirt or how to redeem loyalty points or how to pay for the purchase with cash or credit. That standard alone has almost five hundred use cases. In many cases, including the level of detail contained in all these use cases would make a book overwhelming in its size and breadth.

It doesn't make any sense to duplicate all the incredible work done by the thousands of ARTS participants. Instead, the level of detail included will teach how the standards relate to each other and support the retailer's vast ecosystem. When lower-level details are required, you will be able to dig into the right technical documents from ARTS.

CHAPTER 1

What Is Retail Technology?

In the beginning, the cash from a retail transaction was stored in a cigar box. As one would expect, theft was high. To solve this, along came the cash register. These were pretty handy, but they were mechanical and slow. The next iteration, the electric cash register, was much faster but still a standalone device.

As more computers found their way into cash registers, now called point of sale (POS), retailers wanted to tie them together. The first POS interface standard was a semi–de facto standard from IBM called TLOG. It was semi-standard because there were three different versions. (I'm skipping a lot of history because it is not relevant to ARTS.)

This is where ARTS came into the scene. The industry was getting too complicated to have unique interfaces with all the applications in the enterprise. The cost of upgrading, even with the same vendors, was getting cost-prohibitive. Adding new applications was a herculean effort. In a high-paced, constantly evolving world, this was an inhibitor to the retailer in becoming and staying competitive.

Vendors initially fought standardized interfaces because they mistakenly believed that they would allow retailers to easily move to other vendors. While this sounds true, the cost of learning new applications overrides the expense of replacing someone else's application. In addition, they were limiting sales of upgrades to their own applications.

ARTS developed an extensive inventory of standards to help solve this problem for retail. What is retail in this context? Do the ARTS standards apply to more than one industry?

I constantly hear people say, "ARTS is for retail, and I work in food service (or convenience). It is totally different!"

Let's examine that. Does food service sell items? Yes. Do those items have a price? Yes. Does food service have customers? Yes. So are retail and food service the same? No. Are there things that are different? Absolutely. A food-service establishment is in effect a mini-factory where the items sold are created on the fly after the customer orders the item. But can't the customer order a new set of built-to-order cabinet shelves? The cabinet would have a "recipe" to describe how to build the cabinet. It would have a bill of materials where the parts are identified.

In the end, the difference between these two "factory" orders is basically time. In food service, the time is nearly immediate because the factory is onsite. These kitchen systems are totally unique in food service. This is why ARTS has special support for the unique components in the kitchen environment.

In today's hypermarket, traditional retailers must be able to deal with and support selling shirts, hamburgers, and fuel from the same store. To this end, ARTS has created several standards and has worked with other standards bodies to extend support for these other verticals.

This fundamental decision is in any industry, whether it is hard goods, soft goods, c-store, grocery, or food service. Basically, if people are selling items, then they are exchanging goods for tender, dealing with customers, and enticing them into their business.

Section 1.1: Introduction

We start by exploring the foundation of communicating in technology, the infrastructure. The infrastructure is how systems and applications physically communicate. Think about how many times your cell phone call drops the connection. The infrastructure supports the connection your phone has with the person on the other end. The infrastructure is what keeps dropping the connection.

ARTS has a series of white papers dealing with infrastructure. They build on each other; the first talks about the basic requests and responses model where one application requests information from another, and the responder replies with the answer. It also talks about publish-subscribe models where the sources of the message, called publishers, publish their messages directly to any applications that have subscribed to receive them.

The next white paper covers a concept called service-oriented architecture (SOA) where applications are broken into pieces called services. These services are then choreographed to perform some business function. The beauty of SOA is the way these services can be quickly and dynamically connected to create new processes. This allows retailers to quickly respond to new needs. With a set of SOA services, some of the services can be located locally within the store, and others can be located remotely.

This leads to the next white paper, which describes cloud computing. Cloud computing lets retailers optimize their infrastructure costs without impacting performance. The services defined under SOA can be optimized with respect to where they exist by putting appropriate parts of them in the cloud. Properly deciding which SOA service should belong in the cloud can provide cost-effective, responsive solutions to the retailer.

When smartphones came along, people could access these processes from virtually anywhere. The next white paper describes the various uses for mobile technology in retail. The mobile revolution led to social media, and the next white paper explains the risks and benefits of using social media in retail.

With this foundation in place, we turn our attention to the reason for retail: selling things to customers and making a profit. This part of the book is broken into three sections (with ARTS support for each).

The first step in the path is locating the store. Here's where it gets complicated; what is a store? In today's multichannel world, a store can be a website, a mobile application, a catalogue, or even a traditional physical store. Understanding the relationships between each is important because the retailer must be able to present a consistent look and feel in whatever channel the consumer uses.

The next section follows the ARTS "Consumer-to-Customer Life Cycle Model" technical report. The life cycle describes the phases a customer follows from being in the general population to being a shopper to the important stage of being a customer. Part one of the life cycle sets the stage for getting the consumer into the store. To get consumers into the store, they need to be able to match their desires to what is being sold; advertising answers this question.

Once the consumer is in the store, turning him or her into a customer is the next section. If the consumer is a customer, then there is a loyalty aspect to enticing the customer back into the store. Customer loyalty is covered under the umbrella of targeted marketing.

Section two covers turning this consumer into a coveted customer by selling him or her something. Once a consumer gets into the store, he or she must be able to easily find out where the items they are looking for are located. This involves laying out the store properly. One of the key analytics, to seeing how efficient a retailer's store layout, involves looking at all the paths the customers traverse. If you have areas of the store where no one enters, then those areas are being paid for with no return on the investment. In addition you must then have items properly placed to drive impulse and affinity buying.

The next section deals with the point of sale (POS). This is arguably the most important real estate within the store. Here is where the customer exchanges money for goods and services. As such, today's POS is a very complicated piece of machinery. When ARTS started, the release of ARTS's first product, the ARTS Data Model, supported POS. It slowly expanded to cover the entire store. In version 4.0, the data model expanded to cover the enterprise. Needless to say, a lot of effort has gone into creating standards for all the applications and devices connected to POS.

One way to understand how POS operates is by using a task state diagram. A task state diagram describes the behavior of the system, in this case the POS. It defines the various states of the system and what it takes to move from one state to the next. The POS task state diagram tracks a POS transaction from the beginning through all the stages to the end. All along this path, the POS outputs data containing all the information developed during each phase of the checkout process. The checkout process is very complicated and takes the coordination of wide, diverse engines. It includes everything from the price engine for calculating the prices and applying promotions to the tax engine for calculating the appropriate taxes to the output (POSLog).

Next, the book explains the support ARTS has for calculating and managing making a profit. This includes first reconciliation where the money in the till is balanced against reported sales. There is a discussion about how retailers can determine whether they are making a profit through a set of business intelligence key performance indicators. This includes managing the workforce. The workforce is the retailer's largest controllable expenditure. If there are too many associates on the clock, the retailer loses money. If there are too few associates on the clock, the retailer loses customers. The trick is the balance. To paraphrase a children's story: not too many, not too few, just right.

At the end, the book discusses food service–specific support, such as kitchen systems and forecourt specific support around fueling stations.

This is the first in a series of books around ARTS. Future books will include details not covered in the ARTS-supporting documentation.

CHAPTER 2

What Is ARTS?

Retail technology includes all the systems in a retail enterprise that are necessary for exchanging goods and services for money. For this book, that excludes the accounting side and the human resources side. There are other standards bodies in existence to support those areas.

ARTS is a unique organization. Both retailers and vendors helped create these standards. ARTS produces four different standards: the ARTS Data Model, ARTS XML schemas, UnifiedPOS devices, and a business process model. In addition, it produces a variety of white papers and request for proposals (RFPs).

Section 2.1: The History of ARTS (Association of Retail Technology Standards)

The Association of Retail Technology Standards (ARTS) began in 1993 when several retail CIOs got together to solve a common problem they all had—data. They realized that every time they brought in new software, they had to reinvent the data model. Migrating from the existing data model to the new data model cost a lot of time and energy. If they made a mistake, recovery was expensive and very disruptive to the primary focus of selling items. They wanted to solve the problem that retail data was the same—no matter what kind of retail business you were in.

With this fundamental concept, they released version one of the ARTS Data Model in 1997.

ARTS's Mission

ARTS's original mission was "to enable the low-cost, rapid deployment of technology in retail by reducing integration efforts through platform-independent, vendor-neutral standards." This mission remained in effect for over a decade.

In 2011, the mission was expanded. "The mission of the Association for Retail Technology Standards (ARTS) is to develop best practices, technology standards, and educational programs through collaboration and partnerships that will enable retailers, their vendors and suppliers to conduct business globally. ARTS standards, products and programs are dedicated to fostering innovation, improving shopper experience, and increasing retailer efficiency."

ARTS Boundary

ARTS has a boundary. It works primarily inside the walls of the entire retail enterprise. When ARTS started, there were standard bodies working in the business-to-business arena. There were standards in the financial arena, in the human resources arena, and for managing purchase orders. From this recognition, ARTS developed a basic premise that it won't create a standard where one already exists.

This means that the various standards can overlap where they touch at the boundaries. ARTS tries to work with these other bodies and has developed a close relationship with GS1 and the North American Food Equipment Manufacturers (NAFEM).

Why Have Standardized Interfaces between Applications?

Years ago, before ARTS, interfaces between applications were unique. Integration was time-consuming and expensive. Vendors would say they owned the data stored in their application. This wasn't true. They didn't sell the shirt; the retailer did. When ARTS came along and standardized the interfaces, there was a paradigm shift; all of a sudden, the retailer was in charge.

When a vendor has his or her own interface to an application, a retailer can't easily change to a competitor. Therefore, once a vendor has the retailer as a customer, it is very difficult to change to a competitor. That logic sounds great, and it permeated the industry. The fallacy with that argument is that the future is limited. Here's why it makes upgrades in terms of applications and capabilities almost impossible to do. Any changes have to be coordinated with all parties involved. Because of this, the retail industry was slow to react to new ideas, keeping them behind the kind of enhancements that could make them more profitable. On top of that, it made maintenance upgrades a nightmare.

With the advent of service-oriented architecture, cloud computing, and mobile and social technology, another paradigm shift is underway. The customer is being put in charge. The customer now defines the items being sold, and their prices, capabilities, and characteristics. Most importantly, they decide where the items are sold.

Interoperability

For two applications to communicate, several things must happen. At the lowest level, an infrastructure must be in place where messages can be sent quickly, reliably, and securely. Once a connection has been established, they must talk the same language. If one is using French and the other is talking in English, communication will fail. If they are both talking the same language but are using different definitions for the same terms, again communication will fail. To speak the same language, the same set of business practices must be in place. ARTS enables two companies to communicate using the same language with the same definitions.

Section 2.2: ARTS Product Lines

ARTS started with its data model. Next, ARTS joined the National Retail Federation, and along came the UnifiedPOS group, which standardized interfaces between the devices, such as scanners, printers, and POS. Next came what is now called ARTS XML to standardize interfaces between applications.

RFP templates reduced the time and cost of buying equipment. The latest product line, Business Process Modeling (BPM), came along to show how to tie everything together. If one reads everything ARTS has published, that person will have a college education about retail technology.

Section 2.2.1: ARTS Data Model

The ARTS Data Model represents a place to store all kinds of operational data. It started as a POS data model; it became an enterprise data model in version 4.0. In version 7.0, the ARTS Data Model had its largest update in its history; the ARTS Data Model was expanded to cover the entire consumer-to-customer life cycle. This book is based on that model. In 2013, the ARTS Data Model is divided into roughly sixty-four subject areas with 188 views supported by 885+ entities and 6,600+ attributes.

Arguably the most important data is the information around a sale of goods and services to a customer. In ARTS, this is called a retail transaction; it is stored in the ARTS Data Model in a subject area called POSLog.

Section 2.2.2: ARTS UnifiedPOS

At the time all this was going on, a group called OPOS led by Microsoft was creating standardized interfaces for devices, printers, scanners, etc., connected to the POS and based on a programming concept called COM (com object model). In response to this, people from the Java programming world were creating a competing standard called Java-POS. To make things more interesting, people in Japan created a group called OPOS-J. These groups came to ARTS in 1999 to create a unified interface standard where only these implementations (Java, COM) were different. This new standards division in ARTS became UnifiedPOS; version 1.14 released in 2013 covered thirty-six different devices.

Section 2.2.3: ARTS XML

Along came a new emerging interfacing protocol from the World Wide Web Consortium (W3C) called Extensible Markup Language (XML). In 2000, ARTS created REDEX (Retail Data Exchange in XML). Active Store was another active group defining XML messages for use in retail. Active Store and ARTS formed a cooperative called IXRetail for International XML in Retail. Eventually, IXRetail subsumed the work being done by Active Store. For years IXRetail existed until the name was changed to bring it in alignment with the ARTS Data Model name, and it became known as ARTS XML. It is known by that name today. In 2013, ARTS had twenty XML schemas covering over 90 percent of the interfaces in a retail enterprise—a task no other standards body has every attempted.

Section 2.2.4: XML versus ARTS Data Model

ARTS foundational standard was a logical data model. The primary use of a data model is to capture information and put it in context with other information. For just this reason, the ARTS Data Model has been very widely adopted by the retail community. In addition, it provides the foundation for a number of vendor applications. When the discussion is around master data management, the ARTS Data Model provides a ready source for defining the master data.

Literally thousands of individuals and companies have been involved in the creation of the ARTS Data Model. What does this mean? Individuals in every company become experts on their companies' products. So the people who have been involved in the creation of the ARTS Data Model have brought their expert knowledge to the table. That means the ARTS Data Model contains expert knowledge in a wide variety of segments, verticals, etc. This knowledge cannot be attained any other way. There is no other source of knowledge about all of retail.

Many companies have gotten tired of trying to tie all the vendor-specific data models together, and because of this expertise embedded within the model, they have moved to implement the ARTS Data Model.

When XML came along a few years later, ARTS was able to leverage this new technology to define the interfaces between applications. With the ARTS Data Model defining the data at rest, this new thing allowed ARTS to define the data in motion.

Section 2.2.5: ARTS RFP (Request for Proposal)/ITT (Invitation to Tender)

ARTS started because several retail chief informational officers (CIOs) recognized that they all used the same set of core data. They simply used it differently. The same thing is true when buying equipment and applications. There is a core set of features and functions that are applicable to all of retail. If ARTS could identify that subset, it would dramatically reduce the cost of getting an RFP/ITT on the street. The retailer could then focus on what makes it unique.

In around 2003, the NRF's CIO Council was looking for a way to reduce the cost of putting a detailed request for proposal (RFP) (invitation to tender [ITT] in Europe) on the street. RFPs are very expensive for a retailer to produce and for a vendor to respond to. By having a very good starting point, the costs could be reduced, and the quality could be increased, providing a better product at a cheaper price.

The first RFP ARTS developed was for the POS. It proved to be very cost-effective. The first company to use this RFP got a POS RFP on the street in twelve man-days, saving them around $100,000. Another CIO said that he could justify the cost of purchasing the RFP template from ARTS by just trying to organize the first meeting.

Conversely, having a core set of features and functions allows vendors to prepare responses to this core set and focus their efforts on what makes them unique. One chief technology's officer (CTO) for a well-known vendor went through the RFP and highlighted capabilities they didn't support in their application and had those scheduled to be added. In 2013, ARTS has nine different RFPs; the last is cloud computing.

Section 2.2.6: ARTS Technical Reports (White Papers)

ARTS took on thought leadership by accepting the challenge represented by emerging technologies. When a new technology arrives, each vendor uses his or her own terms to describe the new technology. This is great for the vendor, but it is bad for the retailer. Because of the different definitions for the same concepts, retailers were not able to effectively compare implementations. Through a series of white papers, ARTS endeavored to create one set of terms with one definition to clarify new technologies. It is fascinating that they all build off of the foundations of ARTS (data model, XML, and UnifiedPOS).

ARTS walks a fine line. The implementations are fully in the realm of the vendors. ARTS tries to standardize the explanations without prescribing how to build the products.

ARTS's first white paper was on infrastructure. It described various communication methodologies. It is fascinating that these methodologies became the foundation for later white papers. In addition, it identified various pieces of data required at the infrastructure level.

The next white paper described service-oriented architecture, which breaks applications into services. Once there were a bunch of services, the cloud computing white paper arrived. Cloud computing allows retailers to put selected services in the cloud. When the services moved to the cloud, the next white paper covered the mobile revolution. Once everyone had mobile devices, social communication took off. The ARTS Social Blueprint explained how retailers could take advantage of the new communication channel.

Section 2.2.7: Business Process Modeling (BPM)

Why Business Process Modeling Technical Report V1.0.0

The thirty-nine-page "Why Business Process Modeling?" technical report was released on November 29, 2010. There were eighteen individuals from fourteen different companies involved in creating this release. The technical report provides a common set of descriptions around the terms used in the BPM world. It talks about the value of investing time and effort into defining the business processes in each company. It also discusses the BPM journey.

BPM Discussion

When ARTS XML started, ARTS set out to identify the interfaces that needed XML messages defined. This challenge was attacked from a wide variety of directions. After all, trying to understand the business was not new. To help guide the XML development, a retail model subcommittee was formed with the author as its chair. To do its work, the retail model subcommittee utilized everything from mind maps to functional decomposition to existing models. The first version of the ARTS Retail Reference Model was created in 2001. The end result was a scary-looking diagram, but it helped guide the development of the XML schemas.

ARTS has an extensive set of standards that touch many areas of the retail enterprise. For years, the ARTS XML standards explained the payload that was delivered from one application to another. Originally, this payload was a description of the business logic that created the

XML message. As ARTS matured, the need to see how to use ARTS standards in context of the business problems they were able to solve became obvious. This led to the need to define the process choreography in order to understand what standard to use and when. ARTS started including Business Process Modeling Notation (BPMN) diagrams alongside the use cases.

This was fortunate because over the years, with each use case, a portfolio of BPMN diagrams was developed. When the SOA, cloud computing, mobile and social technical reports came along, they led to ARTS putting these BPM diagrams together in one business process model.

After producing this series of white papers, it became apparent that a cleaner model was needed to communicate how all the ARTS products fit into the retail landscape. At the same time, the tools were improved to make the modeling easier and more dynamic. In addition, because of the wide support for retail contained within the ARTS standards, ARTS decided to model the entire enterprise starting at level zero. Level zero is the highest ARTS retail reference model. As a result, the ARTS Business Process Model was born in 2013.

It must be noted that ARTS is focused on the operational side of the business. There are other standards organizations that deal with other areas, such as finance or human relations. Although these areas are included in the ARTS BPM model, they are there for completeness only, and there are no plans for ARTS to model them below level two.

CHAPTER 3

How Does a Retailer Communicate?

When ARTS XML started, there was much heated discussion around what ARTS was. Were we about plug-and-play or message format? It was finally decided that a retailer with infrastructure in place would not change just because ARTS chose a different one. This discussion around infrastructure still crops up regularly because people need a mechanism by which to deliver messages. ARTS compromised and wrote its first white paper on infrastructure.

Most of this book is around the payload. This chapter covers the series of infrastructure white papers. It discusses how applications communicate to accomplish a variety of tasks related to helping retailers efficiently operate and ultimately communicate with their customers. These white papers build on each other—one enables the next—to help dynamically and inexpensively communicate with the retailer's most important asset, the customer.

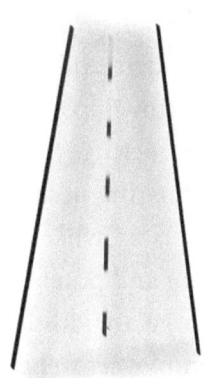

Interoperability requires two major components, the payload and the infrastructure. The payload is basically the business content where one communicates what is happening; an example is

Figure 1: ESB   selling a shirt. The infrastructure is about delivering the payload safely and securely. It has two components, the application status layer and the infrastructure layer. A vast majority of ARTS's XML work is about defining the payload. To address the infrastructure side, ARTS has written an evolving series of white papers to clarify the issues.

ARTS started this discussion by describing the various types of infrastructures and the attributes necessary to support them in the infrastructure white paper. The white paper covered the fundamental connectivity, the request/response, and publish/subscribe models. It also went over the data that one needs to support an infrastructure.

When service-oriented architecture (SOA) came along, applications could be split into a set of services. Conceptually, these services are a set of building blocks. Just like a set of building blocks can be put together in as many ways as one can imagine, these services can be choreographed to accomplish any process one can imagine (theoretically). The beauty is that this choreography can be somewhat dynamic, enabling a business to change quickly in response to market demands.

Once a set of services is defined, one needs to properly locate these services. In the past, retailers needed to build out an infrastructure large enough to support the company during the Christmas season. This meant there was a lot of excess capacity sitting idle for ten months of the year—until cloud computing came along. By properly placing the appropriate SOA services with an Internet-based cloud computing company, retailers can reduce infrastructure costs during the non-Christmas part of the year and elastically scale up as demand increases throughout the year, such as during the back-to-school sales.

Smartphones created another revolution. To help understand this, ARTS put together the mobile blueprint. Mobile blueprint sits on top of—and takes advantage of—the content in the infrastructure, SOA, and cloud computing papers. Mobile computing is fascinating because it impacts consumers by allowing them to shop and buy from wherever they are. It enables retailers to market directly to existing and potential customers. All of a sudden, the consumer was put in charge. In addition it allows the retailer to communicate directly to store employees to help better manage the store.

The smartphone and retailers' ability to talk directly to customers led to the next paper on social retailing. The paper established three goals for social retailing. The first was managing your brand by helping establish the brand, fortifying it with marketing messages, and changing or influencing the brand. The second goal was increasing your customer base. Traditional marketing practices still apply here.

Social media is another channel for reaching customers. The paper's third goal was increasing loyalty by moving the customer from brand awareness to considering your brand—and being loyal by preferring your brand. These goals drive the strategies and tactics necessary to accomplish them. In today's world, customer relationship management will be—and should be—the top priority of retailers. It is too easy for customers to shop elsewhere.

Section 3.1: The Infrastructure White Paper

The first white paper was about basic connectivity models. It discussed the request/response model where one application would request another application to do something. The other application would respond with the answer to whatever was requested. The white paper also discussed the publish/subscription model. In this model, one or more applications would subscribe to messages from one application. Whenever this application published something, all those who subscribed would receive the message. The paper takes the publish/subscribe model to what is the main thing being done today—the enterprise service bus. In this ESB model, everyone is a publisher, and everyone who needs the data subscribes to that application or message.

ARTS Infrastructure Technical Specification V1.0

The forty-five-page infrastructure white paper provides a solid foundation for understanding the infrastructure requirements, including various protocols from pub/sub to request/response. It also discusses in detail the necessary content of a header. This information is used in the ARTS header today.

Infrastructure Discussion

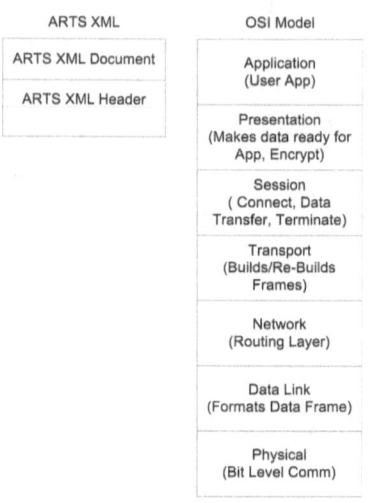

Figure 2: ARTS to OSI Mapping

To be able to communicate among two or more applications, three areas of infrastructure come into play. First, there is the message payload between applications. This payload contains the information necessary to run the business (sales, inventory, customer, etc.). Second, there is the status of the applications trying to use this message information. Is the database application up? The third area deals with the raw physical network connection. This third area is covered under the lower levels of the Open Systems Interconnection (OSI) model (ISO/IEC 7498-1). As such, the lower levels are out of the scope of ARTS.

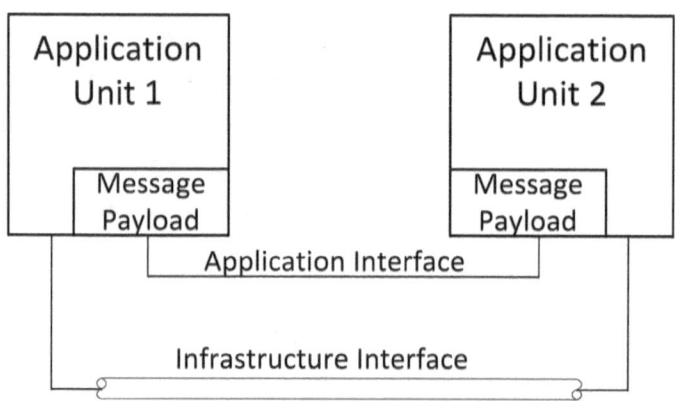

Figure 3: ARTS 3 Level Messages

The Message Payload

ARTS has created a large number of XML schemas that cover over 90 percent of the operational interfaces. These will be discussed when they come into context throughout this book. There is extensive support for almost all message payloads used in a retail enterprise.

The Application Status Layer

This layer covers information shared between two applications about the status of each application. It is quite normal to send an XML message with sales information to an inventory system, only to have the message rejected. It is not rejected because there is something wrong with the message, but there is some problem with the receiving application. An example is when a database is down. The sending application requires feedback about the cause of the error in order to take appropriate recovery steps.

The Infrastructure Layer

The infrastructure layer is the physical connection between the two applications, and other standards bodies handle it. Periodically ARTS will recommend specific network layer protocols, such as web services for the UnifiedPOS devices, but vendors and retailers normally handle it.

Section 3.2: Alternate Communication Protocols

Section 3.2.1: Request/Response

Request/response protocol is one of the original protocols for communicating between applications. With this protocol, one application asks something from another application. It could request a piece of information or request the application do something. The receiving application responds with the result of its action.

Its significance for ARTS is around the service-oriented architecture (SOA) paradigm. As will be discussed later, in SOA architecture, an application is divided into a set of services. To perform some function, these services can be choreographed into higher-level services. These higher-level services can use a request/response protocol to perform the choreography.

Section 3.2.2: Publish/Subscribe (Pub/Sub)

While request/response is a tightly coupled protocol where one application talks directly to another, a pub/sub model is a loosely coupled model where the publisher puts a message in a queue. A middleware piece (a message broker) takes the message off the queue and securely guarantees delivery to the subscribers to the message. Adding a canonical message model by using one of ARTS XML standards for the message creates a powerful, flexible infrastructure.

There is, however, one drawback. A message broker is a single point of failure. To overcome this limitation, the idea of putting a message broker at each application interface was born. This is now called an enterprise service bus (ESB).

Enterprise Service Bus

An enterprise service bus is an infrastructure architecture where every application plugs into a backplane, much like how circuit cards go into a computer backplane. Each plug-in slot is called a node. The messages are routed from the source node to whatever receiving node registers to receive that message. The key to making this work is a canonical message model on the backplane. ARTS XML makes this possible.

In a traditional architecture, one of the major challenges with applications is managing upgrades. Whenever one application gets upgraded, all the applications that interface to it may also have to be upgraded. The beauty of the ESB model is that individual applications are isolated from each other. This way, one can remove or update one application without having to do anything with the other applications on the backplane (just like changing circuit cards).

The ESB with ARTS XML standards provide an incredibly powerful implementation of this pub/sub model. All retailers should seriously investigate whether this model is correct for them. With this model, each application is independent of all other applications.

Section 3.3: Service-Oriented Architecture (SOA) Process

The SOA process enables tighter coupling between the boardroom and the associates on the floor. Making this happen requires managing the entire process from top to bottom. Under SOA, the people at the top can express their strategies for their businesses. The business analysts can interpret these strategies into a set of tactics. Working in conjunction with the enterprise architects, these tactics can be choreographed into processes with a set of services. The associates on the floor can use these processes to help run the business. From top to bottom, the components of this transformation are called the SOA Stack.

Section 3.3.1: Service-Oriented Architecture (SOA)

Not all applications are good at all things. Ideally, the retailer would like to buy the best parts of several applications, put them together, have them talk to each other, and create a hybrid application whose synergy is better than any of the pieces. For this to happen several things have to take place; first, the services (action preformed) have to be clearly identified. There has to be a standard way of interfacing with the service, and they need to use the same data.

In the infrastructure white paper, ARTS described the basics of connecting applications, and it remained constant for years—until service-oriented architecture came along. Traditionally, applications came as one big set of functionality. If retailers liked most of the functionality but wanted to change only a part of it, they were required to upgrade or replace the entire application. In terms of people, processes, and equipment, changes were very expensive. The idea behind SOA was breaking the big application into pieces called services. Retailers could keep the parts (services) they liked and upgrade or change the parts (services) they didn't like or that didn't meet their needs. The result was that any change was much smaller because most of the application capability stayed in place. This had an exponential impact because since the changes were smaller, fewer other applications were impacted by the change. Any problems (and there always were problems) were smaller in scope. Everybody liked that! The other significant part of SOA was enabled and the speed of change was increased. Basically, SOA allowed retailers to change directions on the proverbial dime.

ARTS XML SOA Blueprint V1.2.0

To help explain what the SOA process was all about, ARTS created the SOA Blueprint. The third version of the ARTS SOA Blueprint was published on December 25, 2008. Thirty individuals from twenty-six different companies were involved in the creation of the blueprint. The 109-page blueprint included discussions about the approach to SOA, the SOA technologies, how ARTS supports SOA, and the path to SOA.

Figure 4: SOA Services

SOA Discussion

With traditional retail architecture, changing the direction of an enterprise was much like changing the direction of an ocean liner. It took a long time, and it made a big, slow circle. With SOA dividing an application into a set of services that could be dynamically strung together, retailers could be as flexible as a motorboat. To make this happen, the SOA Blueprint described how enterprise architects could encapsulate business functions into reusable SOA services.

Many people grew up with a collection of blocks of wood of various shapes and sizes. They would use creativity to build as many different objects (houses, barns, cars, etc.) as their imaginations could come up with. These reusable SOA services (blocks) allowed retailers to dynamically put them together to build whole new sets of processes (houses, barns, forts, etc.)

These building blocks could be choreographed to perform things never envisioned by their creators. Software applications became building blocks that were used by enterprise architects to dynamically respond to changes in the retailing world.

Notice that SOA defines the business as a set of IT services, or it defines the IT services as a set of business functions. In other words, one enables the other. The business mission is implemented by dynamically stringing them together.

The key to dynamically integrating these services is having a standard lexicon and standard interfaces to the services. The lexicon ensured that everyone who used a term was using the same definition as everyone else. The ARTS Data Model provided this and more. It also provided the relationship between the terms. Now one knows what things mean, one needs to be able to dynamically plug services from potentially different vendors together much like plugging different devices into a USB port. That required a standard set of interfaces. ARTS XML standards provided those interfaces.

As more systems arrived in the store, it became more expensive and difficult to update the applications in an enterprise, particularly if the company is spread out around the world. Even if a retailer is able to get a single application rolled out to all their stores, it was normal to have different versions among the various stores. Creating a homogeneous enterprise was very difficult. SOA made it easier for retailers to be agile and to respond quickly to changing landscapes.

In addition, companies are always buying, merging with other companies. Integrating all the disparate systems is a nightmare, takes a long time, and is very expensive. The acquired companies can be migrated to the corporate master data, but that normally takes years. In the interim, the company still wants to make money. SOA architecture dramatically reduces the problems, but it doesn't eliminate them.

Another cool side effect is defining the processes so that customers can use their preferred channels to get a consistent experience through other channels. An example is when a customer purchases an item on the web for pickup in a store. On the way to the store, the customer finds another item on his or her smartphone and adds it to the order. While picking up the items at the store, the customer can purchase other items in the store and has the same experience during each interaction.

Section 3.3.2: The SOA Stack

The ARTS SOA Blueprint defines an SOA stack to help understand SOA's impact on an entire enterprise. The stack starts in the boardroom when they define the business strategy. The next key to the puzzle is governance. The rules and regulations are defined and managed to keep control of this beast. ARTS has a couple of papers to help, including the SOA Best Practices and XML Best Practices.

The next key is the enterprise architects. These people arrange the model, strategies, and tactics into a set of business processes using business process modeling. The next piece is the service-oriented architecture.

The SOA architecture describes a hierarchy of services by starting at the bottom with stateless entity services. Entity services simply perform a single function. Entity services can be connected together to form task services. Task services and entity services can be choreographed to perform a process. They get built into Provider and Consumer services where one provides information and the other consumes this information to accomplish some task. These service types are choreographed to accomplish the logical business processes.

The SOA Blueprint discusses how to communicate these services at the infrastructure level by using either web services or Representational

State Transfer (REST). The message payloads of these are the ARTS XML schemas.

The last key in the puzzle is master data management. Because information can come from services provided by many different sources, having one set of standard terms, definitions, and relationships is mandatory for a robust SOA implementation. Of course, ARTS supports master data management with the ARTS Data Model and Data Warehouse.

One fascinating byproduct of ARTS XML schema work is how it is required for a well-defined SOA architecture. It is almost as if ARTS knew SOA was coming when the XML work started in late 1990s. This is especially fascinating because SOA wasn't even on the horizon when ARTS started the XML work.

ARTS XML schemas provide a standardized canonical message model for connecting SOA services. The ARTS XML messages determine what the message payload component of the interface looks like. When people build services with ARTS XML schemas before they start, they know exactly what the interfaces should look like.

SOA Governance

With SOA comes great flexibility, but with great flexibility comes the potential for great chaos. With SOA, all one has to do to create a new business process is choreograph a set of services into the new business process, possibly creating one or more new processes. Before long, everybody will want to create their own choreography, resulting in a large number of single-use processes built to solve particular problems.

On top of that, people change jobs, leaving behind all the processes they created and used. Without proper governance, the number of permutations can overwhelm the system, leading to the creation of duplicate processes. SOA governance defines the rules needed for effective management of the SOA environment. Governance provides the ability to lasso the chaos. Governance defines who, where, when, and how people create and use the business processes orchestrated from the underlying services.

Business Process Modeling

One of the key benefits of SOA is the ability to quickly orchestrate new business processes. This is initiated with business process models. One of the tools used by enterprise architects to communicate these business process models is business process modeling. BPM models the choreography of the processes retailers use to conduct business. After retailers choreograph the business processes, they can tie in the appropriate services identified in SOA work. As described earlier, ARTS is continuously developing and refining a foundational retail BPM to help with this step.

Enterprise Service Bus

An enterprises service bus is the next piece of the puzzle. As discussed earlier, an ESB provides a standardized backplane that allows services to be dynamically and securely added and removed as needed to support the defined business process.

**Figure 5:
Enterprise ESB**

Adding ESB to the architecture creates the two major components identified in the infrastructure paper. Both the XML payload and ESB delivery mechanisms are identified. From here plug-and-play of services is almost achieved. With the standardized interfaces supplied by ARTS XML, SOA services can be added, moved, upgraded, and removed from an ESB independently of each other.

Now with an identified ESB and a dynamic set of services, people can quickly respond to guidance from the boardroom. They only have to speak the same language, the next piece of the puzzle, with master data management.

Canonical Message Model

On the technology side, SOA doesn't need an ESB, but it works extremely well with one. Making the ESB work properly and efficiently requires a standard set of message data. All applications either directly use this set or map the data. ARTS XML schemas provide this canonical set of master data. This way, applications on the ESB don't need to know about the format of the other applications' messages. The terms from every application and device are converted to the standard master data terms at the integration point when the message is put on the bus.

This becomes particularly important when one moves these services into the cloud. In a cloud environment, these SOA services can be located anywhere and shared everywhere. Having a canonical message model and a MDM environment gives a company the flexibility to dynamically change the location of the services as new needs arrive.

SOA Best Practices V1.2.0 Technical Report

ARTS SOA best practices describe the patterns, such as the naming convention, granularity considerations, and lexical and syntactical principles, used by ARTS to create a set of SOA service schemas derived from the ARTS XML schemas. These schemas represent the canonical message model necessary to plug SOA services together. ARTS publishes these SOA-enabled schemas. The first was an SOA implementation of POSLog called Retail Transaction Interface (RTI). Later customer, tax, self-service interface, item, price, inventory, and location services were added.

Section 3.4: Master Data Management

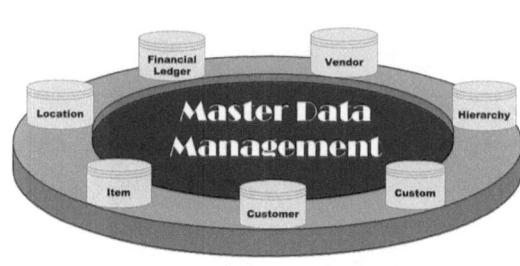

Figure 6: Master Data Management

Data can be divided in many different ways in retail. Some data is used to make decisions (master data), and other data is the result of those decisions (transactional data). Master data provides one set of common terms and relationships that is used to understand the entire enterprise. In order for the people running the organization to make intelligent decisions, they must clearly understand what is happening in their company. Master data is the foundation of making intelligent decisions. Master data management is the process of getting that one set of common names, terms, and relationships.

The heart of making SOA work is having everyone speak the same terms with the same meanings. The next piece of the puzzle is making sure the content is understandable. This can be challenging to modern retailers. In today's retailer/vendor environment, retail stores are bought and sold on a regular basis. This makes integrating and understanding the content from these dynamic sources difficult.

Master data management is the Holy Grail. It provides one version of the truth. Every retailer strives for it, but as one gets closer to achieving it, the powers that be buy another company, and the integration begins again. When a retailer has a few stores, understanding the business is easy. But as the retailer grows, acquires, and/or merges with other companies, understanding the business becomes almost impossible. This is partly because each acquisition has its own way of doing business, using its own terms.

For example, one company may call the thing they sell an item, and another will call it a product. These represent two different names for the same piece of merchandise. If the CEO wants to find out how many shirts were sold, does he or she look for items or products? What if the CEO doesn't know about both terms? Eventually, the terms may migrate into the common lexicography, but at the start, they need to be integrated into the new organization. To do that integration, there must first exist a common set of well-defined master data. It may sound simple, but many companies have yet to conquer this concept. This is where MDM comes into play. Upper management only uses one term, and all variations are mapped to this term.

There is another side to this dilemma. Sometimes a company is a collection of related—but distinctly different—concepts. In this case, the unique terminology of each individual concept may need to be kept unique to the concept. How do the people at the top make intelligent decisions? They need to have the unique concept terminology mapped to the enterprise master data terminology.

MDM is one of the kingpins of the service-oriented architecture stack. This is the only way to effectively integrate applications/services from a wide variety of different vendors and sources.

ARTS MDM RFP

MDM is about having a consistent, accurate, and timely set of the company's core data. This is where ARTS comes into play. First, ARTS published an MDM RFP to help retailers purchase an MDM solution. The ARTS Master Data Management RFP provides a set of features and functions that comprise the MDM solution. These features and functions start with identifying what MDM is for retailers, and then it defines the master data management process by profiling the data, cleansing it to remove duplicates, extracting unique pieces, exporting them to the proper database, and loading them into the database.

The RFP also talks about the steps to help retailers migrate from their current model to a master data model. It starts with an extract/export/load; selected data is removed from the existing database, and the data is cleansed. Data cleansing standardizes, transforms, synchronizes, and rationalizes the data, removing duplications and inaccuracies, and getting to the single truth of item information while maintaining an accurate audit trail.

Once clean data exists, it is profiled to see where it fits in the MDM model. Profiling uses techniques such as frequency analysis or pattern analysis to identify whether the information is unique, and where the data fits. It is necessary when the data comes from a variety of sources. Once the data is cleansed, the business rules for translation are applied to improve the data quality before insertion in the MDM data model.

The MDM RFP also identifies seven core sets of master data: item, customer, vendor, location, hierarchy, financial ledger, and custom data. This doesn't mean there aren't other MDM areas since retailers will have information that they define as master data. ARTS's primary support for defining master data is the ARTS Data Model. The data model provides extensive support of master data in the seven core sets of master data and many others. In one view, most of the ARTS Data Model is master data. If one is looking to communicate master data, then the ARTS XML schemas can be considered as master data in motion.

MDM in an SOA World

There is a slightly different view of master data when one talks about the SOA world. Here, the master data can be the canonical message model used to integrate all the different services. Having a canonical message model allows retailers to plug and play all the services into one enterprise service bus. ARTS's support for the canonical messages is all the ARTS XML schemas.

Implementing MDM is a key component of migrating to SOA and should be incorporated into the path as early as possible. One of the major keys to SOA is to have this master data management structure solidly in place. The only way services can interoperate is if they have this one version of the truth. Another approach is to use the ARTS Data Model as the canonical model. If both services use the ARTS Data Model as this foundation, the integration between these services is much, much easier. There will still be differences, but they will be minimal.

This doesn't mean that all of MDM must be implemented before migration can happen, but it does mean that MDM is an integral part of the path and should be phased in at the appropriate time with the appropriate level of detail. Ignoring it or delaying it can have serious consequences to the success of the SOA effort.

In the real world, services are tailored to optimize unique businesses. So an integration layer is needed. ARTS has the answer. ARTS Data Model defines a common vocabulary to be used at the enterprise level. If an ESB is used to integrate the systems, then the ARTS XML schemas can provide a canonical message model for integration on the ESB with the ARTS Data Model being the canonical storage model. This means that the messages created at the local level can be translated to the canonical enterprise message model. The translation is one of the capabilities of the ESB and occurs at the point where the application connects to the ESB. This puts all messages in the same context model and makes them understandable.

Section 3.5: Cloud Computing

Figure 7: Elastic Scaling

Cloud computing is one of the most significant concepts for reducing retailer costs. As with most new technologies, understanding what it means is challenging. To help clear the mystery, ARTS created a cloud computing white paper to describe the cloud environment and a cloud computing RFP to help buy a cloud solution.

The RFP divides the technology world into three groups, Information as a Service (IaaS), Platform as a Service (PaaS), and Software as a Service (SaaS). The content of the IaaS group deals with the physical hardware, the servers, the networking, and the storage. The next level up is the PaaS group. This level is comprised of things like middleware, databases, and development tools. The top level is the SaaS group, which is composed of things like business processes, customer loyalty, and collaboration tools.

Cloud Computing Technical Report V1.0.0

The sixty-four-page cloud computing white paper was released on December 12, 2009. There were twenty-four individuals from twenty-three different companies involved in creating this release. The white paper teaches about cloud computing. It talks about different kinds of clouds and gives guidance on what should go where. It describes the relationship between SOA and cloud computing. It talks about the costs of cloud computing and how it provides an enormous savings to retailers. In finishing and to alleviate retailers' fears, it covers security, reliability, availability, and accountability.

Cloud Computing Discussion

Black Friday is typically the day after Thanksgiving (US holiday) or the last Friday in November. Black Friday got its name because traditionally it was the day of the year when retailers became profitable.

What does that imply from an IT perspective? During this short time frame after Black Friday till the end of the year (the Christmas season), retailers needed an enormous amount of computing power; this computing power is sitting mostly idle for the rest of the year. That has an enormous cost. To reduce this expense, cloud computing came along. Cloud computing allows retailers to effectively and efficiently control costs by rapidly expanding and contracting computing capacity as needed. It does this by allowing retailers to "rent" the computing power they need from a cloud provider using the Internet.

When ARTS created the SOA Blueprint, cloud computing was just beginning. It turned out to be next logical step. Under SOA, an application gets split into a set of services. These services can be properly located, some local and some in the cloud, to maximize usage while minimizing cost.

Figure 8: Virtual Computers

Virtualization

Cloud computing leverages a concept called virtualization. Virtualization has been the enabler for mainframe multitasking operating systems for a long time. In its most basic form, it is the technique of simulating a physical computer in memory. Each "computer" is simulated in what is called a virtual machine. These virtual machines can actually run anywhere by simply changing their base location. To the retailer, it looks like a physical machine that is exclusively theirs.

Besides being able to be located anywhere, the beauty of a virtual machine is that computing power can be dynamically added as the need arises, and other virtual machines can be added to solve multiple copies of the same problem simultaneously. Conversely, computing power can be dynamically scaled down when excess power needs are reduced. This characteristic is called elastic scaling. The financial benefit is the lack of a need for capital expenditures. You only pay for what you use in what is called a consumption-based model.

Automated provisioning of infrastructure services allows retailers to add these virtual machines as needed without third-party interaction. Provisioning is done automatically through a website or possibly an app on a cell phone.

On the cloud vendor side, by having clients in virtual machines, the cloud provider can efficiently utilize its resources with a technique called multitenancy. The provider runs the client's virtual machines in one or more physical machines and/or databases. That keeps the costs down and takes advantage of the economies of scale while maintaining data security.

Cloud Types

There are three types of cloud computing architectures or places where these virtual computers may reside. Starting at the store, the first type of cloud is called a private cloud. The private cloud puts the virtual computers under the control of the retailer in their own "environment." This is analogous to a datacenter, although the physical computers are located in the cloud provider's eco-structure. Part of the SOA services identified earlier will need to reside locally in the private cloud.

The second type of cloud is the other extreme; in a public cloud, all the virtualization is located at the cloud provider's infrastructure. The third type is a hybrid cloud where part of the cloud is public, and part is inside the retailer's infrastructure. In this case, some virtual computers are private, and some are public. In the hybrid model, the challenge is figuring what services fit into what cloud.

The fundamental reason that stores exist is to sell things to customers. The infrastructure can't get in the way of this fundamental concept. Because of that, some of the mission-critical services must exist in the private cloud. The technical report provides a list of considerations one must make when deciding what service belongs where.

Section 3.5.1: Cloud Computing RFP

ARTS Cloud RFP V2.0

The second version of the ARTS Cloud Computing Request for Proposal (RFP) was released on September 1, 2011. It added PaaS and SaaS to the first version's IaaS features and functions. When working on the second version, an interesting observation occurred: the features and functions needed to purchase an IaaS solution were the same set of features and functions needed to purchase a SaaS or a PaaS solution.

Each cloud level provides an extensive list of the features and functions around security, audit and compliance, performance, availability and support, reliability, migration, monitoring, manageability, interoperability, capacity, and scalability.

Section 3.6: Mobile

ARTS Mobile Retailing Blueprint V2.0.0

The second version of the mobile retail white paper was released on January 4, 2011. There were more than fifty people involved in writing this paper, and another seventy-three people participated in the creation of this 185-page white paper. This paper was a collaborative effort between different standards bodies, each covering a different portion of the mobile ecosystem.

Figure 9: Mobile

The white paper discussed different mobile application technologies, including how mobile and social relate. Then it dove into the most important areas, starting with mobile marketing. It identified advertising, customer service, providing product information, loyalty, and target marketing. It then moved to mobile commerce and discussed how to include the mobile device in the selling process. The term is now called *mPOS* for mobile POS. There is a subset discussion around the use of mobile payments.

The final major area where the mobile device impacts retail is mobile operations. The paper discussed how to embed the mobile device in many of the phases of store operations. Finally, the paper discussed implementation strategies and gave advice on how to move from a non-mobile world to a mobile world.

Mobile Retailing Discussion

In SOA, an application was broken into a set of SOA services. Those services were then choreographed to accomplish a process. Cloud computing allowed for a cost-effective, efficient organization of those services by properly placing the services in the correct type of cloud. This allowed easy, secure access anywhere. While all this was evolving, a new enabler came along; it was called the smartphone. In the ARTS Mobile Retailing White Paper, the two collide.

In the early years of the twenty-first century, people carried around cell phones, personal device assistant (PDAs), and navigation units. At the time, it was apparent that someone would someday put them all into one device. Along came Apple, and the rest is history. Today's mobile phones have more computing power than full-blown computers did a few years ago. This has led to an explosion of apps for these mobile smartphones. These mobile devices are insidious, and they are working their way into every aspect of retail.

Go anywhere, and you will see people interacting with their mobile phones. Smartphones are everywhere. As the pace of life increases, people have less time to stroll the aisles of their favorite retailers. To help them manage their time, they surf the web or access an application with their smartphones whenever they have the time. They can order items directly or decide where they will shop.

For many, shopping is a social event. Teenagers shop with friends, a pattern that stays with them for life. It used to be that teenagers would go to retailers and browse with their friends, trying on this and that. Because they didn't have any money, they would leave. Later, they would take their parents to the store to buy what their friends had agreed upon. Mobile retailing has taken this to a new level. In today's world, those friends no longer have to be present to help with the shopping. They can do it through social media on their cell phones.

To this end, retailers are required to integrate their social media/mobile strategies with their customer relationship management (CRM) database to profile customers more accurately based on their interests and behaviors, and to help manage future two-way communication.

The theme of this book is getting consumers into your store, turning them into customers by selling the something, and making a profit. How does that relate to mobile? Mobile is another channel to do the same thing. Mobile marketing is about getting consumers into your store. In this case, the store may not be a traditional brick-and-mortar store. It may be a website or a mobile application. Mobile commerce covers turning consumers into customers by selling them something. Finally, mobile operations are about making a profit.

Get a consumer into the store. Retailers cannot sell if there isn't someone to buy. Mobile marketing allows retailers to reach out to customers and future customers in ways no one envisioned just a few years ago.

In printed media, the research shows that it takes one year for an advertisement to generate solid returns.[1] For the first few months, the reader skips over the ad; as time progresses, the reader starts to recognize and read the ad. Eventually, a desire for the product grows; after about a year, the ad starts generating sales. With the Internet, this cycle is dramatically reduced, and mobile marketing puts the communication (advertising) right in the customer's hand.

Funeral homes are typically set up to handle 250 guests of the deceased.[2] For years, this was the maximum size of most people's

---

[1]   Sarah White and John Woods, *Do-It-Yourself Advertising*.
[2]   Richard M. White Jr., *The Entrepreneur's Manual*.

sphere of influence. If a customer had a problem with retailers, their complaints would reach a maximum of 250 people. Today, that sphere has morphed into a social network that consists of thousands, most of whom they've never met. The scope and size of this network makes it imperative that retailers diligently monitor these networks. They must proactively respond in a positive manner; if done intelligently, they can turn negative experiences into positive ones. If handled properly, retailers can increase their brand awareness. However, a word of caution, ignoring or responding in a negative manner can be disastrous.

Retailers must also protect their brand images. If an individual is dissatisfied with an interaction with a retailer, he or she will voice this dissatisfaction via social media. Using a mobile device, the person can quickly reach out to social networks with any concerns. This takes constant monitoring by the retailer to keep a misunderstanding from exploding and going viral. To handle this many retailers are setting up groups to specifically monitor the various social media channels.

On the other hand, mobile marketing provides an unprecedented way to establish and maintain a personal relationship with customers. Through mobile marketing, the message can be tailored to an individual customer. Customers can be provided extended information about items they are interested in. They can be provided access to reviews from people called influencers.

In the past, there were influencers who reviewed what stars wore to award shows. Based partly on those reviews, the public would go buy cheaper outfits that resembled the stars' outfits. Social media through mobile marketing has taken these influencers to a whole new level. Influencers review individual items, and they review the entire shopping experience. This gives retailers opportunities to reach customers with tools that are only limited by creativity. For example, promotions can be targeted to customers who are currently in the store. Unlike the old way where a sign was put on the floor and everyone in the store could see it, which is still a very effective way to convert consumers to customers, the promotion can be sent directly to customers.

People like having fun and talking with friends. It's almost impossible to walk down any street without seeing someone with a cell phone glued to his or her ear or text messaging his or her BFF (best friend forever). Retailers need to figure out how to tap into these social relationships. There are a number of ways to do this, including sharing, games, and group buying. These will be further explored in the section on social media.

Mobile Commerce

The next step in turning consumers into customers through mobile commerce is enabled through two techniques: a traditional browser or an application downloaded to a mobile device. Because of the display size limitations, both techniques require a special reduced user interface.

All the traditional ways of selling to consumers come into play here, starting with a catalog where the shopping basket is filled. Next is the payment process where the shopping basket is priced and eventually purchased. Finally, the delivery mechanism kicks in, and the purchased items are shipped to the customer.

Mobile Operations

Wireless devices are not new to mobile operations; they have already been in use for over twenty years in retail stores and distribution centers. What is new are the associates having their own mobile devices. The expansion of available devices in the store has a significant positive impact on increasing productivity, maintaining inventory accuracy, and reducing expenses. It enables store managers to more efficiently utilize the labor force by having direct contact for communicating instructions.

Mobile Point of Sale

Historically, a POS was a heavy piece of equipment with all sorts of wires hooked to all sorts of peripheral devices, printers, scanners, etc.

But thanks to this mobile revolution, those wires are being cut and the heavy piece of equipment is migrating to the smartphone. Mobile point of sale (mPOS) is this latest iteration in the life cycle of a cash register.

James Ritty owned a saloon in Dayton, Ohio, and wanted to reduce employee theft. In 1879, he invented the first cash register. It was a simple device that basically kept a running total of the sales. Next, paper was added to create a permanent record of the individual sales and to print receipts for the customers. The electric cash register eventually came into being when electricity was added. With the advent of the microprocessor, the POS was invented. Somewhere along the path, the Internet involvement drove a non-traditional point of sale. The smartphone led to the mPOS.

There are two implementations for most mPOS applications. One method is to access the application through a browser. This technique has been around for a long time on desktop and laptop computers. The other more recent method is to download an application to the mobile device to run the application locally.

There are three ways to run each of these two implementations. First, the implementations can be run on devices specifically designed for this. Line-busting devices are one example of this. Second, they can be run on an associate's local mobile device. The third is to run on a customer's device.

Now one can have a dynamic POS where appropriate components reside in the store while other components reside in the cloud. With a proper infrastructure in place, one can dynamically build a POS based on the phone's location. Think about creating a shopping list at home on your mobile phone, going to the store, and being guided around the store to the items on your list. After you select the brand, you put the items in your shopping cart and have your mobile phone scan the items or read them with a RFID tag. Your mobile phone can interact with the store's pricing engine to give you a running total.

When done, you can approach a payment terminal, which is basically a row of printers. You can pay with your online account or by waving your near-field communication chip–enabled phone next to a NFC reader. Finally, transfer the transaction to the retailer by printing a receipt on any one of the printers or by—being the green person—having a digital receipt sent to your online personal accounting software.

The next piece of the puzzle is paying through a mobile device. Mobile payment or mobile wallet is evolving. All mPayment options have some connection either directly or indirectly to the banking system, but they have different ways of collecting the tender. They start with the traditional credit/debit card through a web browser, moving all the way to near-field communication (NFC) in the store. The ARTS mobile blueprint characterizes browser-based payment as mobile remote payment and POS payment as mobile proximity payment.

Section 3.7: Digital Receipts

Digital Receipt was ARTS first XML schema published in January of 2002. The idea was to provide an electronic copy of the receipt to the customer. However, it was way ahead of its time and languished until the advent of the mobile and green worlds. Today more than 640,000 tons of paper are used in creating and distributing paper receipts in the United States each year.[3]

Making mPOS work requires a printer attached to the mobile device or having the receipt in some digital format. ARTS Digital Receipt is that format. To support the green movement, retailers needed a way to send electronic receipts to customers. To support mobile retail, the digital receipt allowed people to have receipts delivered to their e-mails or mobile smartphones. In one of the mobile implementations, customers can store this information and credit card numbers in the secure area of the chip in the smartphone.

---

[3]   Don Fornes, "Please Kill the Paper Receipt—Updated." *Software Advice.* April 23, 2010.

The ARTS Digital Receipt XML Standard finally came to life. It is rapidly gaining wide acceptance because it allows customers to get their receipts electronically and avoid printing paper receipts.

The environmentally positive ARTS Digital Receipt can be used to electronically transmit paper receipts to customers. This allows customers to digitally track their purchases, managing their finances and taxes. For refund and warranty information, the digital receipt can be used to confirm to the retailer the occurrence of the transaction.

Digital receipts play an important role in customer loyalty. In order to send a digital receipt, one must know how to contact the recipient. That gives the retailer the opportunity to market directly to the recipient. This information adds more data points when the retailer mines the data; an example is determining the effectiveness of a particular campaign or promotion.

For customers, the digital receipt allows them to electronically receive and file the receipt in a particular financial package. Once they have received the digital receipt, they can use it to register for a warranty or return products.

With the merchant storing the POSLog version—and the customer having the digital receipt version—it is easy to match and validate the customer's purchase, no matter what channel of the original purchase.

Section 3.7.1: Digital Receipt versus POSLog

The output from a POS contains a lot of information beyond the physical receipt given to the customer. For example, if an associate logs into the POS to begin a shift, that information gets transferred to the time and attendance application. If money is taken out of the till to give to a window washer, it is reported. To communicate all that could come from a POS system, ARTS has created an XML schema called POSLog. Since the ARTS Digital Receipt is an XML implementation of a physical receipt, it becomes the foundation of POSLog. POSLog tracks and records everything that can be done at the register. Digital Receipt was deliberately built as a selective subset of the POSLog schema to enable easy interoperability between the customer's receipt system and the retailer's transactional system.

While POSLog is the granddaddy of Digital Receipt and is used to communicate a vast amount of internal information within the retail enterprise, the Digital Receipt schema was developed with a substantially different usage in mind. The result, therefore, is different, even though the basic subject is the same—the recording of items and payments in a retail sales transaction.

The Digital Receipt can be used to deliver promotion information to the consumer, i.e., how many points they've acquired in this transaction. It can be used as a proof of purchase for returns, rebates, or manufacturer registration. It can be imported into the customer's personal or business finance application. In the end, it can eliminate paper receipts. POSLog can do everything from recording transactions to cash drawer openings to reconciling the tills at the end of day or shift. POSLog can be considered the heart of retail, and Digital Receipt is the heart of communicating content to customers.

Section 3.8: Social Retailing

ARTS Social Retailing Blueprint V1.0.0

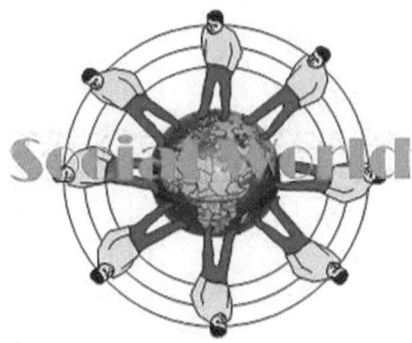

The Social Blueprint was released on January 10, 2012. There were twenty-two individuals from twenty-one different companies involved in creating this white paper. It contained four major areas: goals, strategies, tactics, and social network alignment. In the goals area, it discussed managing the brand image, increasing the customer base, and increasing loyalty. It also discussed three strategies:

Figure 10: Social World

1. *Listen, understand, act.* Listen to what customers are saying, understand their needs, and act to satisfy them.
2. *Attract and influence.* Familiarize customers with the brand and convey its lifestyle and value.
3. *Engage and involve.* Include customers in the conversation, and make them feel like part of the brand.

Social Retailing Discussion

Today almost everyone has a mobile device; the next piece of the puzzle is social networking. People are able to communicate with whomever, whenever they desire, and however they want. This phenomenon has caused a fundamental change in the way people shop.

With this shift, customers take charge. How do retailers adjust to this new paradigm? Social media is a very cost-effective method of gaining, maintaining, and communicating with customers. Retailers must expand their marketing to include this new media.

The ARTS Social Retailing Blueprint discusses social media at three traditional business levels: goals, strategies, and tactics. The goals are divided into three areas: enforcing brand image, getting more customers, and increasing loyalty. These goals are further subdivided into three strategies: listening, understanding and acting; attracting and influencing; and engaging and involving. These three strategies are divided into nine tactics: sentiment/chatter analysis, targeted advertising, user-generated content, check-ins, social graph analytics, crowdsourcing/co-creation, gamification, f-commerce, social shopping, and group buying. This is where things get fascinating. For example, gamification is using a game to get customers to return more frequently than they were before the promotion.

In spite of the convenience of social and mobile shopping, retail stores will not go away. People still like to touch items and browse the aisles. For example, the author knew this very rich elderly lady who would go to Macy's every day. She spent so much time there that she knew every item they sold. For her, a retail store was a place to socialize.

During the winter, many people will go to the mall just to get out of the house.

Conclusion

Retailers can take an application and split it into a set of services and choreograph those services to dynamically do what is needed for the company to be successful. They can optimize operations by putting the appropriate pieces in the appropriate cloud to balance operational needs with costs. The next step is accessing those capabilities anywhere via mobile devices. Finally, retailers can reach out to their customers through social media. Once retailers are able to communicate, the next step is what they communicate. The remainder of this book is about the content of that communication.

CHAPTER 4

ARTS Definitions

In the airline industry, so that pilots from all over the world can understand each other, they all speak English. The same is true in retail; for applications to properly communicate, they must have one definition for their terms. In the past, there were as many definitions for retail terms as there were companies. This was a huge roadblock for interoperability.

ARTS needed to create definitions for many concepts used in retail in order for the standards to make sense.

Section 4.1: Voids versus Cancel versus Return Life Cycle

In retail if you want to start an argument, ask what does "a cancel" mean and what does "a void" mean. You can almost guarantee one side of the room will talk about a cancel as before completion of a transaction, and the other side will say it occurs after the completion of a transaction. To solve this dilemma, ARTS has defined what it means for ARTS. This is an important concept. For ARTS standards to be consistent, ARTS has to use the same terms and definitions throughout. If vendors select the opposite definitions for their work, that is their decision, but they won't be in alignment with the standard.

ARTS has defined that an item can be canceled before a transaction has been both tendered and delivered, basically while the operator is still scanning items.

A major POS vendor would hold the just-finished transaction in memory and not write that transaction to the POS log (a TLOG) until the next transaction was begun. This would give them the opportunity to void the transaction before it was written to the log. They called this void a "post-void transaction." Many other vendors, without knowing the history, misused this term. ARTS supports the concept of a post void but would prefer it not be used. It holds no value in today's POS environment.

Once a customer finishes a transaction, i.e., tenders and receives the items, and wishes to "remove" an item from the transaction, ARTS calls this a void.

Traditionally, EOD reconciliation occurs where the POS transactions are reconciled against the money in the till. Once this reconciliation is completed, the results are sent above store to be included in the financials. After this happens, "removing" an item is called a return.

Section 4.2: An Item or a Product or Product Content Management?

In ARTS, an item is basically something you inventory and sell. It is the foundation of the ARTS Data Model. Products are things that are evaluated to include in the future in the inventory and then sold. During the product-development cycle, the retailer needs to track them and not get them involved with the entire item life cycle. As such, they need a different identifier. ARTS decided to call these items "under development" products.

Section 4.2.1: What Is a Product?

In ARTS, a product is basically something that is still in development. A product ID is used to track the product throughout the product-development process. Once the retailer accepts a product for selling, an Item ID is assigned to the item. At this point, the item can be acquired, inventoried, and sold.

Products have many of the tracking needs of an item, but they are not uniquely identified by the same Item ID. This is because items have a broader life cycle than products do. While choosing a new or updated item, many products are evaluated. Changes are made to the development product and reevaluated, which leads to different versions of the same product. While generally speaking, once it refers to a specific item, it becomes an item.

Section 4.2.2: What Is an Item?

While a product is something that might eventually be sold, an item is something that is sold and tracked in inventory. The concept of an item is very broad and covers basically anything sold. The reach is from food items to apparel to big-ticket items. It can be supplies or services. It also includes items that can be used in supporting the store; for example, a broom can be taken off the shelf and used to clean the store floor or the broom can be sold to a customer.

Section 4.2.3: How Is an Item Identified?

Before centralized inventory systems, each store kept track of its own inventory. To help with this, each store manager assigned a number to each item in their inventory. The name for this number was stock-keeping unit or SKU for short. To further deal with the limitations, all large blue shirts, no matter the brand, would have the same SKU.

As one would expect, a SKU in one store would not reference the same item as that SKU in another store. Along came centralized inventory systems and the need for unique identification for the same item became very important. GS1[4] came into being by creating a

---

[4]   www.gsl.org.

standard identification system for all items in the store called a Universal Product Code (UPC). These are the bar codes on each item and are scanned into the register. A couple of problems eventually arose. First they're running out of UPC codes. Second, the retailers want to track items in the supply chain. To solve these problems, UPC codes expanded to become Global Trade Identification Numbers (GTIN).

GS1 has recently added a Global Location Number (GLN). GLN is used to uniquely identify locations. The location number uses the GS1 company prefix, a location reference, and a check digit.

ARTS supports all these different numbers and others, such as MUZE from the music industry. MUZE is used to uniquely identify digital entertainment content.

Retailers need to be able to track most items at the lowest level possible. ARTS calls this standard identifier an Item ID.

Traceability View

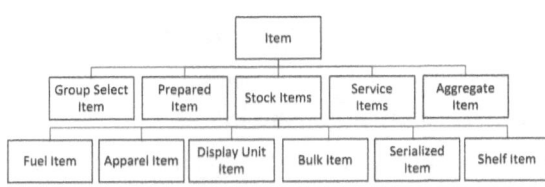

Figure 11: Item Hierarchy

Items could be aggregated in a variety of ways. For example, from a traceability view, there are government requirements around food safety. To support this traceability need, ARTS can track items by the lot number assigned to a group of items generated from one single item. For example, a side of beef gets carved into many cuts of meat. If there is a problem with any one of those pieces, all the related pieces need to be identified so they too can be recalled.

Retailers are creative; they can sell items in almost any way imaginable. Because an item is a multifaceted retail enterprise asset that can take on a variety of different merchandise handling, presentation, pricing, and targeted customer properties and attributes, ARTS has chosen to represent the varied nature of the items handled in a store with a subtype model. The ARTS Data Model is built around five classes of items. These classes are then further subdivided.

Section 4.3: Item Descriptions

Stock View. The largest class is stock item. Originally, this was tangible merchandise stocked by the store. The customer would go into the store, take the item off the shelf, and purchase it. This is still the largest model. In today's e-commerce world, stock items may not be physically stored by the store; they can be shipped directly to the consumer.

Aggregate View. When items are grouped together to be sold as one item, ARTS Data Model normalizes this as an aggregate item. One example is a food-service combo. Each of the items in the combo can be sold separately or they can be put together and sold as one item.

The term combo is where general retail and food service differ. In general retail, the collection is called a kit. Because these terms are so common in both, ARTS XML schemas use both terms; understanding which to use requires understanding the context in which it is used. The data model normalized the term into an aggregate item.

Group Select Item View. The last item class is a group select item. It represents a set of items, only one of which will be chosen by the customer at the point-of-sale. For example, if the customer brings a cup for a "Twelve-Ounce Soda" to the POS and fills the cup at the soda dispenser, that group represents the set of items "Twelve-Ounce Coke," "Twelve-Ounce Pepsi," or "Twelve-Ounce Sprite."

Recipe View. The next type of item is a prepared item. When an item such as a cake or a cabinet is created, it is called a prepared item. The prepared item may be inventoried or created as it is sold. The bulk items used to create the prepared item may also be stock items in inventory.

The item recipe view shows how a prepared item is assembled and made ready to sell, according to one or more recipes. Prepared items are not normally kept in inventory; they are built on the fly as a customer orders the prepared item. However, there are always exceptions. If one is preparing bread or a number of cakes, these can be put into inventory and tracked just like any other inventoried item. The unique aspects around these prepared items include expiration dates and traceability information.

The recipe view was added with the help of one of the largest companies in the food-service industry, but it is applicable to any situation where one builds something. It extends the description view by adding information around the creation of a "prepared item." It's easy to see how a hamburger is prepared, but how about creating a cabinet or putting together a baby stroller. The items used in the recipe are typically kept in inventory. The challenge is reconciling the prepared items sold against the constituent items to evaluate things like inventory turns. Another interesting aspect deals with waste. No matter how good the baker is, some amount always ends up as waste.

Rental View. When an item is rented, the ownership of the item does not change. Or when an intangible service, such as a cleaning or painting service, is performed. These are grouped under the heading of a service item. Stock items may relate to the type of service being offered, such as a floor polisher with a buffer. The rental view deals with items that are rented. These items are characterized by being tracked with a serial number. Because the item is rented, there are terms and conditions associated with the rental. The business needs to track who rented the item; therefore, there is a link to the CRM system.

Labeling View. The ARTS Data Model has two types of labels: one for shelf price labels and one for nutri-facts to cover nutritional properties of food items.

Section 4.2.4: Product Content Management (PCM)

Figure 12: PCM

In today's tactile world, remaining competitive requires lots of visual and audio content to communicate with the customers. ARTS supports this need with a standard called ARTS Product Content Management (PCM). ARTS PCM supports advertising media, the image or video or audio used in the advertising. The PCM Standard enables retailers to get images, audio, and/or video in a standardized format. That can be challenging in today's world where nearly everyone has a camera built into his or her cell phone. Using an image in an advertising environment requires knowledge of what is in the image and how it is displayed. PCM provides this metadata.

In one sense, PCM is a visual equivalent to the physical item. The item schema describes the physical attributes, and the PCM schema provides the visual attributes.

ARTS XML Product Content Management
Technical Specification V1.0.0

On February 1, 2012, version 3.1 of the Product Content Management XML Standard was released. Twenty-two individuals from seventeen different companies helped create this version. The technical specification contained six different use cases further divided into thirty-eight unique scenarios.

Selling an item within a multichannel environment takes two related but different pieces of information. First and foremost, the physical item with all of its characteristics is tracked by its Item ID. Second is a picture of the item so the customer can see (or hear) what the item looks like when it is tracked by its PCM ID.

To sell things, retailers have to be able to entice potential consumers to purchase their products. This is done with advertising through various media: pictures, audio, and/or video. Retailers need the ability to retrieve and share these media, which can come from myriad sources. The ARTS Product Content Management Standard allows this sharing. But just being able to get a piece of media isn't sufficient; you need to know what to do with it when you receive it.

The PCM schema provides extensive information about the content embedded within the media. This three-legged chair includes one leg around information about people, places, and things shown or talked about in the asset. The next leg deals with the entitlements around the asset. That is, when can you use the asset, how can you use the asset, who owns the asset, etc. The third and final leg deals with the metadata around the format of the asset. That includes things like the number of pixels per inch or frames per inch.

Another interesting aspect of the PCM schema is that it enables the user to communicate information about a particular asset, and it allows retailers to search for an asset or request a new asset.

Section 4.4: Promotions and Discounts

Promotions and discounts are two ways retailers use to attract customers and stimulate sales. Promotions and discounts are applied when the items are purchased or returned. To understand their effectiveness and report their impact on the bottom line, ARTS provides extensive support for triggering, reporting, and storing this information.

In retail, there are two different components of a discount or promotion. As with many areas in retail, one part is at rest and the other part is in motion. The at-rest part defines the conditions that trigger the price change to be calculated (the price rules). The in-motion component is the actual price charged for the individual item after the rules are applied. This means items can have different actual sales prices. For example, an item can cost ten dollars for most people, but a 10 percent senior citizen discount can change the price to nine dollars.

Individual Item Discounts

In ARTS, a promotion or discount applied directly to an individual item is called a retail price modifier. They record the difference between the current retail price and the actual selling price, and they tell how the actual price was calculated. These discounts can be either a specific monetary amount off or a percentage off. They can also be generated from a wide variety of rules (as many as retailers can come up with). In order to know which rule was applied to this particular line item, the Rule ID must be recorded. If the operator overrides the price, that must also be recorded.

Sometimes purchasing one item triggers a discount on another item. ARTS has the ability to record the link from the item with the discount to the item that triggered the discount.

An interesting situation occurs when multiple promotions apply to a single line item. The retail price modifier has the ability to define the order of applying discounts. In a situation in which one of the discounts is for one dollar and the other is for 10 percent off, if one applies the fixed discount (one dollar) first and then the 10 percent, the total discount would be less than if applied the other way around.

Transaction Discounts

If a promotion or discount applies to the entire transaction, it is reported in POSLog as a discount line item. It has the same characteristics as a line item promotion, but it is applied to the entire transaction. In some jurisdictions, these transaction discounts are prorated across all the items in the transaction and reported on each individual item. That leaves the possibility for rounding to take place. For example, if a discount is for $1.00, and there are three items, then two of the items report $0.33, and the third item reports $0.34.

The best pricing algorithm is a third type of discount. With this type, the discount applies to only a few different line items in the transaction. To say it another way, four separate items are scanned, and only three trigger the discount. To accomplish this, POSLog has a discount line item that reports the discount and associated rule. It also has an item link element pointing to the three individual items that triggered the discount.

Section 4.5: Calendar

Everything in retail has a date associated with it, starting with each individual transaction. Transactions are aggregated over each day, which is called a business day. Business days are aggregated over various reporting periods. Reporting periods are used for everything from paying taxes to ordering merchandise to scheduling associates.

Furthermore, calendars play a huge role in managing an enterprise. A very large number of key performance indicators are used to judge what a store is doing during particular calendars. For example, the store manager may want to know how sales were for the last quarter. The merchandising department may be interested in how a particular promotion for a particular item went when compared against the period before the promotion. They may also want to know if this item promotion reduced sales of comparable items during the same period. There are labor-scheduling calendars to make sure the right associates are available and have the right skills to perform the jobs needed at the time.

The results of these analyses can be used to schedule associates, jobs, and merchandise. Calendars are used to manage marketing and advertising programs. Basically, they permeate virtually all store operations.

Section 4.6: Tender

There are two ways to account for money: follow the mathematical approach where money can be positive and negative with plus being into the till and minus being out of the till or follow generally accepted accounting procedures where money is real and always positive, only the direction of its movement is different. Either money goes from customers into the till (sale) or from the till to customers (return). By this philosophy, there is no such concept as negative money, and therefore all monetary amounts in the ARTS XML are positive.

The ARTS Data Model is not constrained by the interoperability needs of the XML and is more generic in that it has to support more than one philosophy. To that end, it follows both approaches.

Section 4.7: Privacy

Top Twenty-Five PCI Best Practices V1.0.0

Privacy is a key concern when dealing with customers' personal information. Retailers must do their best to protect this data. There are a couple of reasons for this. First, customers are the retailer's most prized possession. They represent a large percent of the retailer's sales. They will brag about the retailer on their social sites. They are the retailer's best friends. If their customer information gets out, they will turn on the retailer in a heartbeat. Once their trust is lost, so is their loyalty, which will never be returned. In a worst-case situation, this could spell the end of the retailer.

Secondly, there are laws governing what retailers can share with others. Mistakenly giving others this information can result in destroying people's lives. Because of that, huge fines can be levied on the retailer. As a minimum, associates can be fired. There was a famous hacking incident with a credit card processing company. The CIO of a large retailer lost his job simply because his company was using this credit card processor—even though his company was not hacked. There are serious ramifications for not properly securing customer information.

To help deal with the privacy issue and to protect individual's credit and debit cards, the payment card industry created a guideline called PCI. They set about requiring any of their customers (retailers) to certify compliance against these guidelines. In addition, if credit card numbers under the retailer's control were hacked, they were assessed enormous fines. When PCI first came out, it was a mess. The rules for compliance were vague and open to individual interpretation. There were stories of companies passing with one auditor only to fail with the next for exactly the same reason. Note: These problems have been fixed. However there was much confusion. ARTS created a set of around twenty-five questions and answers to help.

The ARTS PCI white paper, released in 2009, was developed in cooperation with the PCI knowledge base with the help of several major retailers and vendors. The list of questions and answers in the paper told retailers how their peers implemented the standards in practice. This great primer showed how others were responding to the PCI mandate.

CHAPTER 5

The Customer Life Cycle

ARTS Consumer-Customer Life Cycle
Model Technical Report

Once retailers have items to sell, they need customers to buy them. ARTS has defined a life cycle for the customer. It starts with the entire population and moves to a customer and on to an ex-customer. Retailers want to move individuals along this life cycle by doing things in marketing and advertising that move the consumer to become a customer.

Section 5.1: Population > Visitor > Shopper > Customer

The customer life cycle starts with the entire population of the world. From this population, retailers want to identify prospects (people who don't currently shop in their stores but could). The next step is enticing these prospects to become visitors to their store or website. Now that they are visiting the retailer's

Figure 13: Customer Target

site, the goal is to get them to start shopping by getting them to put items into a shopping basket.

Until now, they are consumers. The next step is turning them into customers by getting them to buy something. Customers are special! They are hard to acquire and even harder to keep. This is where customer loyalty becomes a key part of the life cycle. Customers have a relationship with retailers that allows their purchases to be tracked. This special relationship allows retailers to focus their marketing dollars toward keeping and enhancing that relationship.

Customers are the source of all glory and the bane of a retailer's existence. Retailers work very hard at getting, identifying, and keeping key customers. For example, one of the largest smartphone companies has a vast part of its income stream from key customers who want the latest smartphones. Whenever they get ready for a new release, they contact their key customers with some sort of promotion, and most will respond.

To that end, there are a number of things retailers can do around the customer. Things can get complicated because customers do not remain static. They move, get married/divorced, change jobs, have children, and on and on until they die. These relationships extend beyond households to include companies, clubs, and organizations to which customers may belong. This makes the management of customer data challenging.

One unique aspect of a customer is that they are known. Because they are known, retailers can build and maintain relationships with them. There are entire companies and products for managing customer relationships. To support integration and storing the information, ARTS has both a Customer XML Standard and extensive ARTS Data Model support.

They support many aspects of loyalty, everything from loyalty programs to campaign management to target marketing. With social media, many more communication channels have risen.

Because of these relationships, retailers can start identifying preferences and needs. Ages, birthdays, and marriage statuses can be used to enhance this relationship. These demographics can be brought into the equation in order to organize customers based on shared buying habits. Of course, retailers need contact information, such as addresses, telephone(s), and e-mail. In today's social world, retailers need to track Facebook and Twitter.

Customer information is the starting point for cultivating relationships with customers. With the shift in retail decision making from sellers to buyers, understanding and responding to customer needs and preferences is essential to retailers' business strategies. Retailers aspire to turn all visitors to their retail business units into key customers. This life cycle model and the importance of capturing and maintaining customer information are central to the ARTS Customer Information View in the ARTS Data Model.

Section 5.2: Customer > Inactive Customer > Ex-Customer

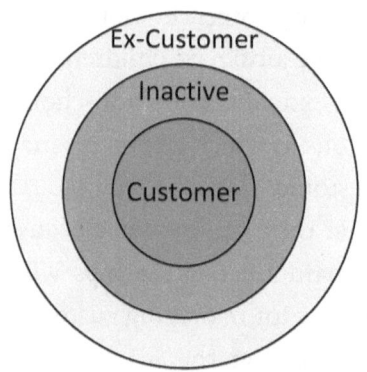

Figure 14: Customer Target 2

Once people cease to be customers, there are still a couple of stages in the life cycle. The next step begins when a customer quits buying items from retailers. At that point, they become inactive. Inactive customers are simply no longer purchasing items from retailers. With proper marketing/advertising, there is an opportunity to return them to the customer stage.

The last customer in the life cycle is the ex-customer. These individuals may be returned to the customer stage, but the chances are not very likely. They may be individuals who had bad experiences or moved out of the area.

Section 5.3: Influencer

Social media has brought into the forefront individuals who impacted a small segment of society in the past. These are the people who review items. To easily understand who they are, they are at award shows to review the clothes that the stars are wearing. Social media has dramatically increased their influence. These individuals may not directly purchase items, but they publish opinions, recommendations, reviews, ratings, etc. Their musings affect all the other types of consumers and customers.

CHAPTER 6

Get a Consumer into the Store

Figure 15: Halter Emporium

In this chapter, ARTS support for getting consumers into the store is discussed. The first step in getting consumers into a store requires retailers to understand what a store is. In the olden days, that was easy. But today, with so many ways for consumers to shop, defining a store is complicated. Consumers can shop on their mobile devices, order on the web, or pick up items in the store. The next step in getting consumers into the store requires consumers to know the store's location. At the same time, they must know that what is being sold is what they are looking for. Basically, they need a reason to enter the store.

Luckily, the group of customers is easier. Since retailers know who they are and how to get in touch with them, a different mechanism can be used to get them to return to the store. This method is called target marketing.

Section 6.1: Why Is a Company in Business?

The simple answer to this question for normal companies is to make a profit. How do they make a profit? They attract consumers and turn them into customers by getting them to buy something. How do they stay in business? They make money on customer purchases. These simple steps are the foundation of virtually every normal company in existence. It doesn't matter if you are selling a shirt or selling an airplane. What does it take to make this happen?

Now that we have an infrastructure, SOA, cloud, mobile, and social architectures in place, we need information. We need information to tell us what customers are buying, how much we have in stock, where our associates are, whether we are making a profit, etc. From now on, we are going to cover all the pieces of information ARTS provides and how those pieces of information relate. Most importantly, how does ARTS support the ultimate goal of making a profit?

Section 6.2: What Is a Store?

To quote *Webster's Dictionary*, a store is "any place where goods are sold, whether by wholesale or retail; a shop." In a generic sense, a store is where customers go to buy something. However, in today's world, one can carry a store on a mobile phone, access it in a browser, or pick up the items by physically walking into a brick-and-mortar building. In effect, a store is no longer only a physical location; it is a virtual location that customers carry in their pockets.

This is significant because customers are now in charge of when, where, and how they shop. Retailers need to be flexible to respond to whatever channel customers choose.

Section 6.3: A Consumer Must Know You Exist

Store Location: Location, location, location—this is the first fundamental of retailing. Before the Internet, a poor location meant a company would inevitably end up bankrupt. However, today many successful businesses have no storefront and no inventory. Many of these successful companies have poor physical locations, maybe even their garage, but a good Internet presence. There are many stories of businesses being run from people's homes. However, for most businesses, location is still the most important initial decision.

Since ARTS focuses on the store after it is up and running, they don't have any standards to support properly placing a store. However, once you have a store in place, ARTS can help consumers find it and navigate through it.

Section 6.4: Locations

There are all kinds of locations in an enterprise. There are locations where inventory is kept on a shelf, in a distribution center, or in a truck. There are locations where things are sold where a workstation is assigned and transactions are created. There are locations where work is performed by stocking a shelf. There are locations where the associates are at any time of day. Locations become complicated because they are not exclusive. For example, in one spot, things can be sold, work can be done, and physical assets can exist.

Physical Location

Once the store physical location is determined, location takes on a different meaning and a different need. It becomes critical to properly running the store. Retailers have to be able to track inventory, assign associates, transfer stock, account for money, etc.

ARTS provides extensive support for communicating the location to properly manage the store. For example, when using a comparison-shopping engine, customers need to be able to find the store that contains the item. When satisfying an in-store customer's request for an item not currently in-stock in store A, but in stock in store B, the associate has to be able to give store B's location to customers.

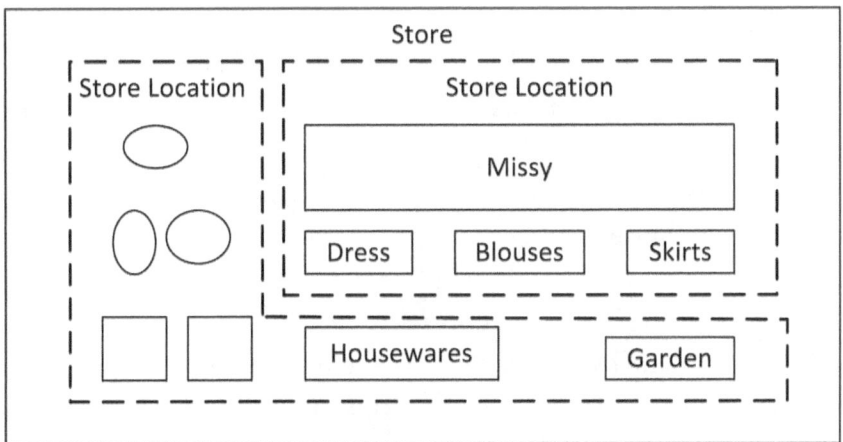

Figure 16: Store Locations

In the mobile world, location takes on a whole new meaning. Customers use the Internet to shop for desired items. They may comparison shop on a competitor's site and check the inventory to see if the item is available. Once they decide where to make a purchase, customers use their mobile phones to navigate to the nearest store. When they arrive at the store, they can navigate to the shelf where the item is.

Location becomes one of the foundational pieces of information needed to run a store. To support this need, ARTS has put location information in the data model and created a Location XML Standard to guide customers to the store—and all the way to the appropriate shelf.

ARTS Coordinate System Insertion Points White Paper V1.0.0

ARTS has produced a white paper discussing all the different types of physical locations that can exist in a retail enterprise. The paper explores all the different location origins in use and reconciles them into a single recommendation. This is challenging because they each evolved differently.

Planograms evolved with the origin at the bottom back left corner, while space planning systems evolved with the origin at the front left corner of the store. The ARTS Video Analytics takes a top-down view from the camera's perspective with the origin being at the top left corner.

Once you figure out where the origin is located, you have to figure are we using a standard right-hand or left-hand Cartesian coordinate system for figuring which direction the x, y, and z coordinates run. The decision was made by ARTS to make the back bottom left corner the origin following the lefthand model. This made the back left corner of the store into the origin for the store. The positive y direction was in the back of the store, and the negative direction was in the store. This seems rather odd, but it makes it easy to map between all the different mapping systems.

ARTS XML Location Technical Specification V1.0.0

Once retailers figure out what they want and how much they want, they get to figure out how to sell it. This includes the store plan (what goes where in the store). This is in part the area of the planogram. ARTS has created a Location XML Standard to help with placing items in the store and helping customers find those items. It is similar to the mapping programs that are generally available on today's smartphones (but for items within the store).

Logical Locations

Originally, ARTS identified a store with a Retail Store ID. Version 4.0 of the ARTS Data Model became an enterprise data model. To identify any place in the enterprise, the Retail Store ID was abstracted to support any place within an enterprise—from the warehouse to the administration center to the retail store. To that end, the term "business unit" was defined.

In conjunction with GS1, a business unit now relates to any location within an enterprise, including the distribution center, administration center, call center, website, distributor, filler, transit cellar, producer, and grower. A business unit is where a transaction originates. A business unit can have a location, such as a postal code to receive mail or telephone to call the store, or geophysical location to get directions to the store.

To bring organization to locations, they can be grouped together in various hierarchies. In the ARTS Data Model, they are called location groups. With their generic natures, they can be organized in whatever manner retailers need for their businesses.

In the normal course of selling, a different type of location is involved. On a daily basis, operators are given a till (cash drawer insert), are assigned to a POS, and begin selling things. During their shifts, they take breaks and the tills are put into repositories. When they return from their breaks, they retrieve the tills and, in the most generic sense, go to a different POS and resume selling. Being able to track what was done—and where—is mandatory if you are going to track associate performance, loss prevention, and till reconciliation.

Section 6.5: A Consumer Must Know What You Are Selling

Section 6.5.1: Advertising

Figure 17: Advertising

No matter how good your items are, customers must know you exist. The first step in selling to someone is to get them to come into your store, visit your website, etc. This is where advertising comes into play.

Advertising deals with making sure, from a customer perspective, there are items available at the right prices with the right guarantees. It communicates that the form and function of the advertised item is easy to use, performs well, and is consistent with the customer's self-image.

Advertising basically involves identifying the target markets, defining the promotions for that market, preparing the advertising media, and delivering the message. There are many moving parts when it comes to advertising. In addition to traditional newspaper and magazine ads, there are ads in motion, such as on television or the radio. In today's world, there are ads on the Internet and throughout social media. All of these take some sort of graphic support. ARTS PCM XML Standard provides access to these various types of media.

In addition to the media having the right advertising, market research is required. To support this research, the ARTS Data Model includes information around customers' demographic and socioeconomic characteristics, including psychological and lifestyle characteristics. Market research also researches customers' attitudes and opinions, awareness or knowledge of a product or concept, intentions regarding purchases, travel, etc., and purchase motivators.

As a part of advertising, promotions are a planned strategy for increasing sales over a short period. They add value to a product by stimulating sales for reasons other than the product's inherent benefits. ARTS has support for all kinds of promotions. From setting them up, to execution, to storing the results and evaluating their effectiveness, starting with the Price Life Cycle Optimization RFP.

ARTS covers the price life cycle by starting with the regular sales price, then moving to temporary price changes (promotion markdowns), and following the end of the life cycle with permanent price changes (markdowns).

Since these promotions are summarized in the data warehouse, retailers can evaluate the overall effectiveness of various campaigns. Of course, ARTS supports all kinds of customer information to support targeted advertising to make sure these promotions get into the right hands. This includes many different flavors of promotions. There are promotions that apply to any customer (10 percent off Tuesday), and there are promotions that only apply to key customers through loyalty accounts and loyalty programs.

Each loyalty program has a set of rules and conditions for customers to get or redeem those loyalty points. The ARTS Data Model has extensive support for the rules and conditions, as well as the points rewarded or redeemed to customers, which is described in the loyalty section.

Section 6.5.2: Merchandise Planning

To plan the merchandise for a particular time of year like the Christmas season, retailers start by establishing the objectives for the season. Some of this is dependent upon what they expect to sell. This input can in part be gleaned from the previous year's sales (not only how much but what kind of items sold). The sales history is stored in the ARTS Data Model. From here the POSLog XML Standard provides the ability to send summarized sales information to be utilized by the sales forecasting application to plan for the season's new goods.

Other components necessary for forecasting include market research to identify what is currently hot in the market (who can forget the pet rock craze a few years ago?). This item information can be stored in the item area of the ARTS Data Model and communicated with the Item Maintenance XML Standard.

Another component is customer information. Retailers need to know who they are, what they are buying, and how much they are spending. The ARTS Data Model contains much support for reporting retailers' customer demographics and purchase history. This information is invaluable for inventory planning and making sure individual stores have a proper inventory mix to support the customers.

Once retailers have figured out what they want to sell, they can query the inventory system to see what currently exists in inventory. They can make sure they have enough inventories to meet the projected demand. This information is contained in a combination of the inventory area of the ARTS Data Model along with the Inventory XML Standard.

Next they can check vendor product availability. Once retailers have established objectives, they need to validate that vendors can provide the quantities in the time frame needed. This may involve multiple vendors in multiple locations. ARTS has minimal support in the ARTS Data Model for vendor information, but this is in the business-to-business world and comes under the standard organization GS1.

Section 6.5.3: Product Life Cycle Management (PLM), Private Label Management

Many retailers are creating their own items called private label products. This generates the need for retailers to manage the product-development process. Under ARTS, this process comes under the heading of Product Life Cycle Management (PLM). As one can imagine, new product development is very complicated. This drives the need for a disciplined PLM approach, especially when retailers begin designing entire collections or lines. To help accomplish this, retailers have a new product-development process and staff independent in the normal sales cycle.

The PLM Business Process Flow covers four major areas. Merchandise planning is where new products are created or selected from the vendor's samples. The vendor's samples are then modified to meet the special needs of retailers. The selected vendor samples are then put through the vendor's production process. Eventually, the products are transformed from a product to an item that retailers sell.

Since these items are not for sale or stocked in inventory, there is no Item ID to track them. So ARTS, to differentiate them from items, calls them products. The impact on the ARTS Data Model is quite significant. Basically, it requires an entire replication of all the item tables plus audits of the factories that might build the products, but it doesn't tie to the financial or operational processes like an item does.

Some products are very complicated, and some steps in the design process may be outsourced. This product development complexity requires the use of Computer-Aided Design (CAD) tools, Bill of Materials (BOMs), detailed technical specifications, 3-D modeling, and the construction of prototypes or samples. Number of products and materials require the coordination of dozens of material suppliers. Since products are tied to a calendar, it gets more complicated when entire lines or multiple products are coordinated with the appropriate calendar.

Because PLM deals with bill of materials, purchase orders, and invoicing, PLM deals with business-to-business interfaces and application-to-application interfaces. Since ARTS is primarily within the walls of the enterprise and must partner with other standards bodies, such as GS1, to provide a complete solution, the enterprise walls are sometimes porous.

Section 6.6: A Customer Must Have a Reason to Enter Your Store

Smart shoppers will research major purchases prior to the actual purchase. They have many tools at their disposal, they can use social media to find out what their friends and influencers are doing, they can go to individual retail sites, or they can use a comparison shopping engine to compare items. To help with this decision to enter a store, ARTS has a standard called Comparison Shopping Engine (CSE).

Section 6.6.1: Comparison Shopping Engine

ARTS XML Comparison Engine
Technical Specification V1.0.0

Figure 18: CSE

On October 6, 2006, ARTS released the first version of the Comparison Shopping Engine (CSE) XML Standard. Nineteen team members from fifteen different companies came together to create this standard. The original meeting in San Francisco had more than forty movers and shakers involved. Interestingly, some of them dropped out to create their own "standard." (If you are a nine-hundred-pound gorilla, you can do this.)

The ARTS technical specification covered publishing images to the CSE. It also validated that the images went to the site and appeared in some consumer-facing media. Prior to this standard, there was no feedback to the image creator. To support validation, this standard managed confirmation of the product information before the product was released. It also had a unique twist—the images could be made available to others for their consumption. Prior to this standard, this information remained with the individuals, but now they could be shared in a standardized format. The standard provided a mechanism for verifying that images had been uploaded. Prior to the standard, images could be lost in a number of ways. The standard provided a mechanism to confirm receipt of the images.

Comparison Shopping

Consumers comparison shop. With today's Internet tools, comparison shopping allows customers to find out who has the best product at the best price or find the best price for the same product. These comparison-shopping engines are fueling Internet purchases. People without a lot of time are using these to make purchasing decisions before they ever leave their houses. On the other side retailers, large or small, can effectively compete and sell their products on the Internet.

However, getting reliable information in a timely manner was difficult at best. The communication was inconsistent, and the format of the data was all over the place. This was a definitive problem that was screaming for a standardized solution.

On a different note, another problem was that retailers would publish content to a comparison site but have no idea when or if it made it to the site. On top of this, with myriad formats, if you made a mistake, there was no way to know what was wrong. To fix this, retailers and vendors needed to be able to send content to the comparison-shopping engines in a standardized format.

On top of the lack of confirmation, there was no way to provide feedback on the number of visitors or the number of clicks. This key performance indicator helps judge the effectiveness of retailers' online stores and their promotions. The CSE schema gives this kind of feedback.

Comparison-shopping engines providers also benefitted. Multiple product feeds from separate retailers would match up products more consistently, allowing the engines to provide more consistent product comparisons on their sites. CSE IT staff could now spend less time confirming and correcting input data and were able to process feeds faster for timelier product presentations.

Generating consistent metrics data for their many customers would also ease the amount of effort each organization had to spend on demonstrating their business value to customers. Standard metrics feeds allowed for faster decision-making speeds and better justification for marketing dollars being sent to CSEs by online retailers.

This concept has morphed to a concept called showrooming. Showrooming occurs when customers visit a brick-and-mortar store to touch, feel, and try on the items—but not buy it. They go online to purchase things cheaper. Retailers are trying to make showrooming difficult by doing things like putting different UPC codes on their items.

Section 6.6.2: Customer Loyalty

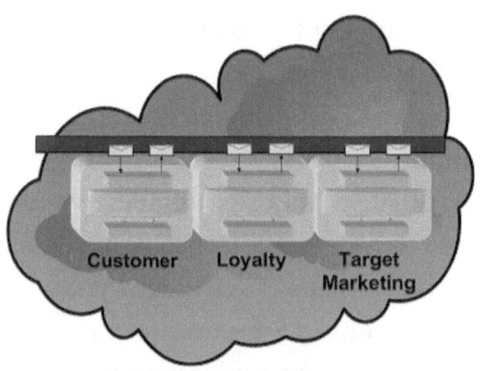

Figure 19: Customer Loyalty Target

Retailers must be able to identify their key customers. Through the loyalty program retailers know the names and addresses of key customers.

Just as dealing with customers is complex, providing them with incentives to remain loyal customers is equally as complex. Remember that we want to turn consumers into customers and keep them. One of the tools to do this is through a loyalty system.

Customer relationships are very complicated. They start with retailers getting individuals to sign up for loyalty accounts. Once their personal information is securely tucked away, the company can regularly communicate directly and personally with each customer. At this point, an anonymous customer becomes a key customer. To further enhance the experience, the key customer can sign up for more than one loyalty account.

As the company starts developing different programs for different times of the year, (back-to-school, Christmas, etc.), they can get these loyal customers involved. This means each loyalty account can be tied to one or more loyalty programs.

If this key customer gets married, the spouse has his or her own set of loyalty accounts. They become multiple owners of all these loyalty accounts. In some cases, some of these accounts are not shared. Something else happens when children are brought into the picture.

Customers are not limited to people; businesses can also be customers. In addition, customers can be employees of a business. To say it another way, employees can be customers through their businesses. When they purchase something at your store, they could be buying it for their company. In that case, they are adding to the loyalty purchases of their company.

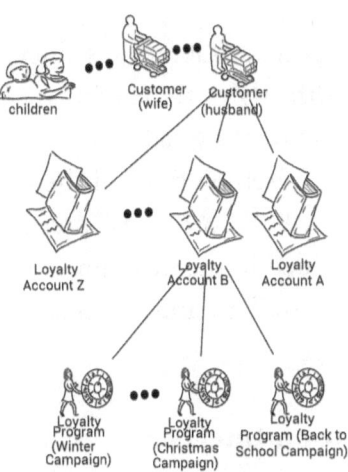

Figure 20: Loyalty

The ARTS Data Model supports the tracking of customers' promotional account activities, and points awarded or redeemed, in the customer promotion activity view. To make these relationships more complicated, there are links to account agreements and terms.

Section 6.6.3: Target Marketing (Customer)

Figure 21: Target Marketing

All these different loyalty programs lead retailers to being able to communicate directly with their most important customers, those who make up a majority of sales—the repeat customer. Target marketing is taking these loyal customers and directly offering them reasons to come into your store. To do this effectively, you must know who your loyal customers are and know their normal purchases and loyalty purchases.

ARTS XML Customer Technical Specification V3.1.0

Customers can sign up for various loyalty programs using the ARTS Customer XML Standard and storing that information in the ARTS Data Model. A wide variety of different systems need this information, and having it in the data model gives them the opportunity to access it when necessary.

With customer history and loyalty information at retailers' fingertips, retailers can target specific promotions directly to those who are most likely to purchase the items. This target marketing reduces the cost of selling items and increases the likelihood of selling more of the items.

From a merchandising perspective, when customers' preferences and promotional account activities are added to the mix, a nice loop is created. Customers buy their items from retailers, and retailers restock the shelves with what the customer desires.

Section 6.6.3.1: Customer Application Interfaces

ARTS has identified a number of areas that use customer information. The interfaces include these (along with a brief description of their uses):

- *transportation management*—where items must be delivered to customers, requiring customers' name and home address.
- *reservation system*—where customers' desires can turn into better customer service by having customers' choices prepared. This way, customers only have to change whatever they want to be different.
- *layaway system*—works without customer information. However, how great it would be to know what item belonged to what customer. Upsell/cross-sell opportunities abound because you know what they bought, and you know they will return to make progress payments.
- *credit-card authorization*—track the type of credit card used. If they use retailers' credit cards, then retailers can provide loyalty options to customers.

- *advertising*—customer information provides guidance on what is the best media to reach these customers.
- *real estate management*—put new store locations where customers (new and potential) are located. Also use demographics to identify new locations.
- *customer account management*—provide a store account to customers and be able to track the amount owed, paid, dates, and account statuses.
- *gift registry*—retailers can track names, event dates, event types, gift preferences, and what was purchased for this customer. This provides the opportunity to cross-sell customers with related merchandise.
- *voucher/gift certificate management*—track the individual(s) for whom customers purchased; how much did they spend and for how long. This provides the opportunity to get in touch with the recipients and turn them into loyal customers.
- *promotion management/target marketing*—provides an opportunity to send targeted promotions to customers based on their purchase histories.
- *contract management*—be able to track items under contract to specific customers.
- *consignment*—tie items customers have for sale in the store.
- *loaners*—track loan items to customers who have them.
- *customer order management*—as a transaction traces a customer's order to delivery, be able to follow what is bought and the order status.
- *merchandise planning*—track the demographics of the customer base. What, when, where, and how are they purchasing? This has significant input for planning the product mix.
- *loyalty*—a key part of the loyalty system, track the points awarded or redeemed.
- *POS sales information*—dates, times, amounts. Provides the source of customer sales information.

- *loyalty redemption*—track what customers purchase and what was paid for with points. POSLog reports this information so the loyalty system can properly deduct the points from customers' accounts. The reverse is also true; when customers return an item they purchased with points, the points can be put back into their loyalty accounts.

- *gift registry*—when customers get married the happy couple registers at their favorite store to help friends purchase wedding gifts. The process typically involves using a scanner to go around the store to identify preferences. The scanner is then read into the store's registry system to record those preferences. When their friends purchase the items on the list, the POS logs the purchase as a gift purchase tied to customers' gift registry. The gift registry can then mark that item as having been purchased. This way, others won't buy the same item. The POS then gives the friend a gift receipt (basically a list of the items without their prices). The friend can give this to the happy couple so they can return it if it is broken, the wrong color, etc. The gift registry view in the ARTS Data Model covers the ability for customers to register for an event, enter a wish list, and then to link purchases against the wish list. POSLog is used to record the purchases against the gift registry. The Digital Receipt can be used to send an electronic receipt to the friend as well as the happy couple.

Traditionally, point-to-point integrations were created for each of these systems, but this can be costly and prone to mistakes. A better solution is to expose "services" that can be invoked by one of more external systems over a network. This is the promise of SOA.

SOA enables retailers to purchase only the services necessary to accomplish the task at hand. To support SOA, the customer schema is subdivided into a set of services: a collection of services to support basic customer information, a group to support loyalty, and/or a group to support target marketing.

CHAPTER 7

Turn the Consumer into a Customer by Selling Him or Her Something

Driving consumers to your store is the first step. Getting them to purchase something is the critical next step. To this end, retailers must take full advantage of the entire shopping area. They must make things easy to find. Many consumers will simply walk out if they can't find what they are looking for. To this end, ARTS has several things that can help. Along the way to the items, they pass many opportunities to purchase other things. The ARTS KPIs can help identify things that belong together to drive this impulse/affinity buying.

Once consumers have shopping carts, it must be easy for them to checkout and securely pay. Besides supporting a large number of different tenders, ARTS created a payment integration white paper to explain how to move the payment process into its own secure box. The circle comes back around by evaluating the transaction to see what is selling and who is buying.

Section 7.1: A Store Must Be Laid Out to Make It Easy to Find Things

ARTS Video Analytics XML Technical Specification V1.0.0

On October 8, 2008, ARTS released version 1.0.0 of the Video Analytics Standard. Twenty-four team members from fifteen different companies came together to build the schema. How this standard began was interesting. Five of the largest retailers in the world contacted ARTS to have a standard created in this area. This was an emerging technology with numerous startups popping up to solve individual pieces of the video analytics (VA) puzzle. These major retailers wanted to get ahead of the curve and have one standard interface established before each startup went in its own direction. The long-term savings for retailers that did not have to deal with everyone's unique interface were potentially enormous.

Video analytics use cases cover things one wouldn't imagine when thinking about the cameras that exist in the store. With video analytics, retailers can evaluate the traffic and the path they follow to evaluate the effectiveness of the store layout. VA allows store managers to check out the various wait times that exist. Any sort of optimization in this area can increase profits by reducing customer wait times.

Of course, there are many loss-prevention capabilities from being able to analyze the content of the store cameras. There are many other things one can do with this information.

Video Analytics

When you get consumers into the store, if they can't find what they are looking for, retailers will fail to turn these consumers into customers.

With the ARTS Video Analytics Standard, one is able to leverage the cameras already in the store to derive actionable information. Video analytics figures out what is happening in the video and turns it into digital content. This content can be evaluated against a set of rules to determine what to do. An example of actionable information is automatically recognizing when a shelf is empty or needs cleanup.

The Video Analytics XML Standard defined two generic concepts for identifying areas and objects in a retail environment. The "area of interest" is the physical area being analyzed for this message. This concept has been leveraged for the Location XML Standard to identify the location of whatever is being reported. It could be meta-data like the store layout, micro-data like in a planogram, a path, or the visual area covered by a video camera.

One of the most interesting use cases deals with watching consumers looking at some advertising, then walking over and purchasing the item in the advertising. As a part of this analysis, they can help figure out the conversion rate. They can figure out when customers look at something and tie this into a POSLog purchase. From there, the areas of the floor can be ranked as to who bought what from where. This information can be fed into the planogram software to help assign items to locations in the store. Video analytics is the only way this correlation can be determined.

One measure of a store's success is sales per square foot. To maximize this, the store must be properly laid out. Customers should move around the entire store. Any place where customers don't enter is a dead zone with respect to sales. How do retailers know if there are any dead zones in their store? The ARTS Video Analytics XML Standard can help. It provides access to information that can be analyzed to identify any areas of the store with minimal or no foot traffic.

Planograms aid retailers in matching product placement with the merchandising plan. These can be as sophisticated as describing what items are sold at what store all the way down to what items are on what shelf and how they are presented. ARTS Location XML Standard aids in locating items within the store.

If the location information is combined with the video analytics information, the store layout can be analyzed at a new level. The customers' shopping lists provide suggested paths for customers. When that is combined with the actual path, the opportunity for store optimization is brought to a whole new level.

The other generic concept is the "object of interest." Objects can be anything from the shopping unit to an item on the shelf to a spill in lane nine. Objects can move through an area of interest, or an area of interest can contain one or more objects of interest. For example, a shopping unit is a group of people who come through the front door together. Typically, they stay together and move through the store as one unit. By watching shopping units as objects of interest, one can determine the various shopping patterns identified in this standard.

Areas have boundaries. In the case of a video, this is the limit of its coverage. A boundary could be the front door. Whenever shopping units enter the store, they are crossing a boundary and entering an area of interest. When they move from jewelry to the men's department, they could be crossing another boundary. Where the boundary exists for each area of interest is important in both the video analytics standard and within the location standard in directing customers to an item on a shelf.

When merging location information with video analytics, retailers can more closely evaluate the effectiveness of layout of their stores. This is called a path of interest.

Section 7.2: It Must Drive Impulse/Affinity Buying

Part of affinity buying is knowing which items sell together and how people move through the store. Therefore, one mixes actual sales with people movement. There is a famous story. An incredibly large retailer noticed that beer and diaper sales peaked at around six in the evening. They figured out that the dad was coming home from work and needed to pick up diapers for the baby. While dads were in the store, they picked up the beer for themselves. The retailer put the two together to make it easier to purchase them both, thereby increasing the sales of both products. Today, they've taken another tactic. They've put them across the store from each other. This requires customers to go across the store; in transit, they might purchase something else.

CHAPTER 8

How Do You Pay for Your Purchase? POS— The Heart of Retail

The discussion around POS starts with its evolution. This puts today's POS in context with its predecessors. The discussion then moves to the major states a POS goes through to sell things to customers. These states are tied to transaction life cycles, which start with customers putting their items on a belt for the operator to scan and ends with customers taking the items out the store. To support and track all the various steps involved in checking out customers, ARTS has created one of its most widely adopted XML Standards, POSLog.

Because POSLog carries all the sales information, it is without argument the lifeblood of retail. Virtually every system in a retail environment uses the data contained within POSLog.

Traditionally, when connectivity above the store was spotty and expensive, these POSLog transactions were transmitted at the end of the day in a batch upload. As the cost of the infrastructure came down— and the need for real-time information grew—transactions were sent above store in real time.

Once the targets for POSLog data were established, the next step was to break a POS down into all its constituent "engines" that are necessary for selling things in today's high-paced world. ARTS has identified a number of these engines and created XML schemas for communicating to these engines and the ARTS Data Model for storing the data.

The final step is how one buys a POS. The first RFP produced by ARTS was the POS RFP called Store Solutions.

Section 8.1: The Evolution of the POS

Figure 22: Transaction

A POS started out as a cigar box from which the cashier would put customers' cash and make change. It migrated to a cash register where individual transactions were recorded on a continuous piece of paper. Periodically, someone (typically the owner) would reconcile the paper against the cash in the cash drawer.

As more and more companies came into existence, a less demanding way of tracking sales and tender was needed. During this period, an electronic record of this information was created, and at the end of the day, the transactions were batched together and forwarded to the home office along with a count of the tender in the till. The home office would reconcile the two to verify that all the tender had been correctly put into the till.

The next iteration evolved with the website and involved near real-time posting of the transaction as soon as the POS was finished. This means transactions were sent one at a time. Over time, the transaction communication was further broken into smaller pieces. With SOA, ESBs, and mobile, each of the pieces was being transmitted as soon as they occurred. This further breaks down to individual line items by building an order and creating a shopping cart, pricing it, and tendering it.

The next evolution, which is still going on, was to integrate all systems in the store to provide real-time information. With new architectures, this evolution changed to what could be termed micro-real-time. Instead of the traditional transaction being published for use by these connected systems, the new breed of service-oriented architectures required the individual components of a transaction to be available as soon as they were entered into the POS. The scope was for everything from a kiosk to a web-based solution to a call-center approach to the mobile revolution.

Section 8.2: POS Transaction State Diagram

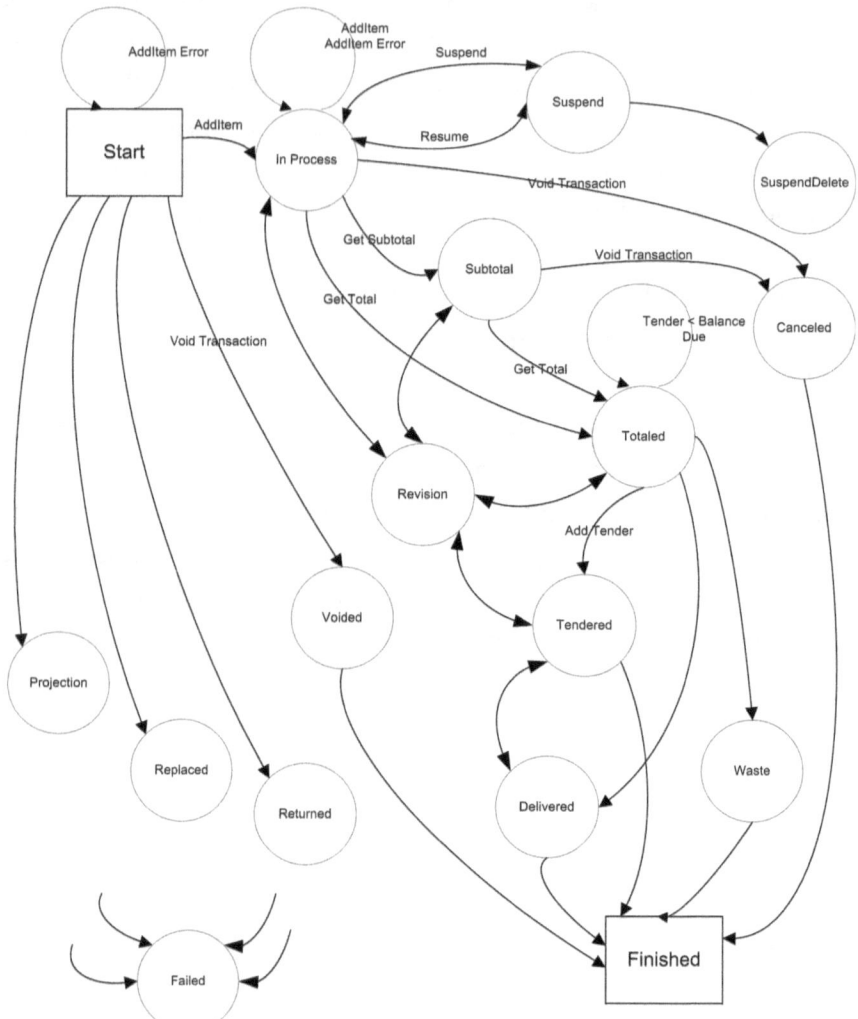

Figure 23: POS Transaction Status State Diagram

Transaction status identifies the various states in which a transaction can exist.

- *cancel*—cancel is used to designate a transaction line or entire transaction that was reversed *prior* to the finishing of a transaction.

- *delivered*—a transaction that has ownership of the listed items transferred to customers
- *failed*—a transaction that has problems forcing non-completion.
- *finished*—a completed transaction (tendered and delivered).
- *in process*—items entered during a one-behind or on-the-fly order entry mode.
- *projection*—a projection of the items needed for a given time period. Used in analyzing the needs, both manpower and inventory, for the store.
- *replaced*—this transaction replaced another transaction. Typically used to correct a problem with the original transaction.
- *returned*—indicates that this is transaction is returned.
- *revision*—this transaction is a revision of the original transaction.
- *subtotal*—indicates an intermediate total is calculated prior to finishing.
- *suspend delete*—deletes a transaction after it has been stored. This has potential inventory implications because food preparations may have begun.
- *suspended*—a transaction that has been stored to be recalled at a later point by the same or different POS during a customer's order. A suspended transaction must be recalled to be changed.
- *tendered*—indicates the transaction was tendered.
- *totaled*—the final total prior to tendering.
- *void*—designates a transaction line or entire transaction that was reversed as part of a finalized retail transaction (tendered and delivered).
- *waste*—reports this transaction as waste.

Section 8.3: Transaction Life Cycle

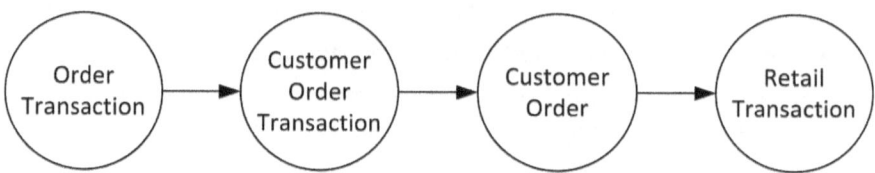

Figure 24: Transaction Checkout Life Cycle

Anytime anyone sells anything, they follow pretty much the same high-level transaction cycle. The way the life cycle is accomplished identifies which steps are included or excluded. For example, at a checkout stand, the only important state is the last one. The other states are compressed in time and don't occur from the customers' perspectives. The other stages are there to support other sales processes.

The granddaddy of all store sales information is contained within what was called the Transaction Level Detail (TLD) of a transaction. Over time, the industry changed. To handle these new needs, extensions were added to the TLD. Today, POSLog is the embodiment of the old TLD plus all the extensions and more. POSLog provides extensive support for every step of the transaction life cycle. A transaction begins when the first item is scanned at the checkout register or the first item is selected on the web. It progresses as more items are added or removed. Next, the transaction is tendered. Finally, the items are delivered to customers. Delivery occurs in a variety of different ways; customers can pick up their bags and walk out the store, the delivery truck arrives at the front door, or the mail delivers the items.

These are all significant steps in the life cycle of a transaction. To support this, ARTS has defined a transaction as having two major components. The first major transaction occurs before the transaction is tendered and delivered. This is called a customer order transaction. The second major transaction occurs after the transaction is tendered and delivered. This is called a retail transaction.

With the advent of online/mobile shopping, a third type of transaction has emerged, the order transaction. The order transaction is created as soon as people start putting items in their shopping baskets. They may never take it to the next level, but they need totals, loyalty, etc.

Most enterprises will recognize the retail transaction as the traditional receipt given to customers at the checkout stand. Normally, the information contained in the retail transaction is uploaded to corporate databases at the end of the day or in real time through trickle polling. It is used to manage the store to update inventory and financial accounts. Retail transaction information can be used to analyze store performance and merchandizing effectiveness. It is truly the lifeblood of the enterprise.

Section 8.4: Transaction

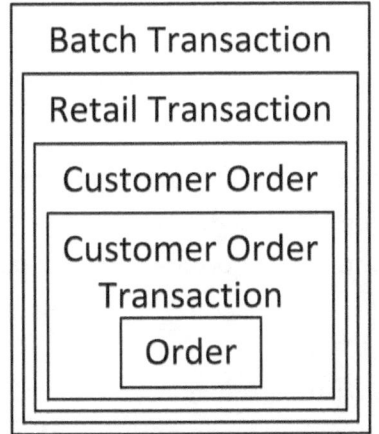

Figure 25: Transaction Hierarchy

Basically three things occur at a POS. First, items are sold to customers. Second, non-sales financial transactions are calculated and transmitted above the store. Third, events are generated to help make store operations run more smoothly.

A transaction in ARTS has many different flavors. To support these various retail processes and more, the ARTS POSLog XML Standard wraps a variety of different transactions under one umbrella.

It starts with an order transaction where individual items are added to a shopping cart. If customers wish to take them to the checkout process, then it transfers to the customers' order transactions. When customers take the order, it adds tendering; if not delivered, it updates this ARTS Data Model customer order. When delivered and tendered, it moves to a retail transaction, which most people would relate with the receipt from the checkout stand.

There are batch transactions for reporting a group of retail transactions to above store systems in one batch, typically at the end of the day.

Then there are transactions like a control transaction, which most people would relate to an event; for example, a drawer limit alert is a notice that the drawer has too much cash in it. Their primary targets are store operations and loss prevention. Then there are tender control transactions, which come into play when actions like money being taken or added to a till outside of a retail transaction. Examples include tender pickup/loan and paid in/out.

Inventory control transactions leverage the POS to report the receipt of inventory. These are primarily targeted for smaller retailers who use the POS for double duty. Finally, forecourt transactions deal fuel information outside of normal sales transactions. An example is a pump test.

Section 8.4.1: Order Transaction

An order transaction occurs during the process of filling a shopping basket. It is a way to keep track of the items selected. For example, when consumers land on retailers' websites and start choosing items to put in their shopping baskets, the order transaction records the contents of the baskets.

Consumers may never purchase anything and may not identify themselves, but there needs to be a way to track the building of the shopping basket. This order may never go beyond there. If consumers decide to go to the checkout and start the purchasing process, the order transaction moves to a customer order transaction. As such, the order can transition through a variety of different states.

During the life of a customer order transaction, retailers have a liability and cannot account for the sale in their profit statements. If customers have not received the items, they can cancel the order with the potential for a restocking fee. For example, they may have a couple of days to change their minds and get their money back, or it could be delivered and then tendered later. In a pizza delivery, the pizza is delivered and then tendered when the delivery person arrives at the door.

Section 8.4.3: Retail Transaction

ARTS has defined that a customer order transaction becomes a retail transaction when it is tendered and delivered. The order of tendering or delivering is not important, but they both must occur to move to the next state. This takes many different scenarios into account. For example, in the web-purchase scenario, the company can't take the sale as profit until the items are delivered, even though the items were paid for when the customers placed the orders. Or the pizza delivery where customers pay for the pizzas after they are delivered, the delivery people return to the store and put the money in the till.

This means a customer order transaction progresses into a retail transaction. A retail transaction, basically the traditional receipt, is a final record of what happened in the interaction with customers. The information contained within the completed retail transactions is used all over the retail enterprise to manage inventory, update the financials, and plan for future purchases. It is truly the heart of retail and is one of the transaction types in POSLog. The output from the POS reports everything related to selling and returning items. In its basic form, it is what appears on the customers' receipt. In it full-blown form, it supports almost every retail system.

There is a situation where a customer order is partially shipped. A POSLog retail transaction is created for the "completed" part, and a POSLog customer order transaction is created for the remaining part. These are sent to the ARTS Data Model where the customer order is updated and the ARTS Data Model retail transaction (delivered and tendered) is added. That is when the income can be added to the financials. Fundamentally, customer order transactions and retail transactions are identical; the difference is their state.

Conversely, it is also possible to have multiple customer order transactions tied to a single retail transaction. Customer order transactions represent a commitment to purchase items. A retail transaction represents the honoring of that commitment and settlement of the transaction with the exchange of tender for the services or products purchased. This would occur in a situation where items are rung up in different departments, like pharmacy and deli, but they are tendered along with other items in a checkout line.

Section 8.4.4: The Traditional Checkout Process

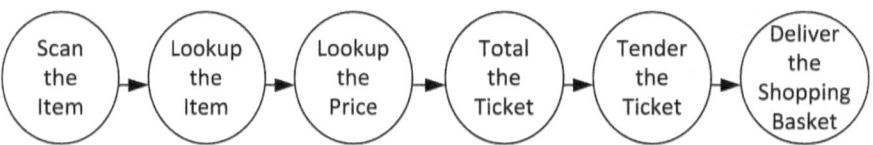

Figure 27: Checkout Process

The central process in retail is the checkout process where customers exchange money for goods. The process traditionally starts when a clerk (called an operator in ARTS) enters the items into the point of sale (POS), typically through scanning. The POS sends the scan code to the item file where the item is verified and maybe converted to a stock-keeping unit (SKU). The item information is sent to the price lookup unit where the price can be calculated. The price is then added to create the total for the ticket. At this point, customers pay for the tickets and take their purchases out of the store. Of course, the web and social media have dramatically changed and expanded this model.

There are many different nuances to this process, dealing with things like promotions, customer loyalty, and different ways to purchase and deliver the items. The variations are too extensive to be covered in one book or even many books. However, ARTS POSLog has the information to cover almost every one.

In a traditional retail store, customers bring the items they wish to purchase to a checkout stand and associates scan the items, take the tender, and package the items. But in today's world, all this has changed. We now have call centers, websites, and mobile buying.

Section 8.5: How to Communicate These Transactions (What Is POSLog?)

ARTS XML POSLog Technical Specification V6.0.0

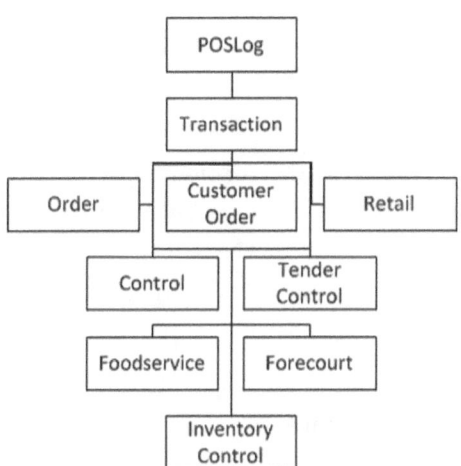

Figure 28: Transactions

ARTS UnifiedPOS, ARTS Data Model, and XML standards are incredibly successful. Retailers and vendors from all over the globe have adopted them. Someone in virtually every industrialized nation in the world has downloaded one or more of ARTS standards.

This is where the ARTS POSLog XML Standard comes into play. POSLog provides the message set necessary to transmit POS information anywhere needed in the enterprise and beyond. This widely adopted, powerful interface has revolutionized the information flow within an enterprise. POSLog enables the new service-oriented architectures to have access to this micro-real-time transaction information. It does so without sacrificing the traditional end-of-day batch processing or real-time transaction message approaches.

POSLog holds the moniker of the most important XML standard ARTS has produced. Getting customers into a store is critical to the success of any enterprise. Once you have them in the store, you must have the right merchandise at the right price at the right time for them to purchase it. A critical piece of information a retailer needs in deciding what customers want is what has sold in the past. Since POSLog is a record of what has sold, it provides a tremendous source of insight for the merchandising system.

On the input side, POSLog records the information retrieved from the various UnifiedPOS defined devices connected to the POS, such as scanners. This information gets converted by the POS with interactions with the ARTS Data Model and is communicated to whatever application needs this information.

On the output side, POSLog interfaces directly to the ARTS Data Model to allow the sales information to be stored. One significant benefit is the ability to mine the information to help make intelligent decisions around how to run the store.

Originally, there was a de facto standard called the TLog. It was electronically recorded, and it was uploaded to corporate systems for processing at the end of the day. When POSLog began, it was simply a migration of the old TLog binary model into XML. But over time, it became apparent that POSLog was much more valuable to all of retail beyond just as a log. That's because the sales and financial information contained within POSLog is the heart of retailing. Virtually every system is somehow dependent upon this information. Today POSLog contains many times the information in the TLog.

As said before during the day, POS provides three major categories of information. The first is what everyone expects (normal transactional data), which is basically a receipt. In addition, there is a host of non-transactional financial, non-customer-facing financial transactions. For example, money is taken out of the till to pay for a window washer, or money is taken in from the newspaper vendor. This type of POSLog transaction is called a tender control transaction. The third major set of information deals with real-time event feeds. These events feed areas, such as store operation or loss prevention, enable them to make timely decisions. It also contains a few minor targeted areas that deal with inventory control, food service, and forecourt.

When the POS reports a sale using the ARTS POSLog XML Standard, there has to be somewhere to store the data. The POSLog area of the ARTS Data Model provides support with a number of different views that reflect the complexity of the POS data.

Section 8.5.1: Retail Transaction

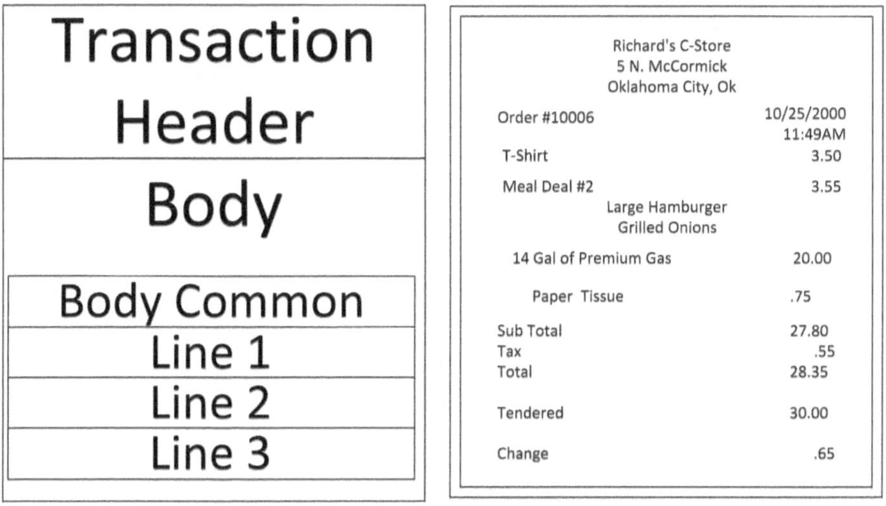

Transaction Header
Body
Body Common
Line 1
Line 2
Line 3

Richard's C-Store
5 N. McCormick
Oklahoma City, Ok

Order #10006	10/25/2000 11:49AM
T-Shirt	3.50
Meal Deal #2	3.55
Large Hamburger Grilled Onions	
14 Gal of Premium Gas	20.00
Paper Tissue	.75
Sub Total	27.80
Tax	.55
Total	28.35
Tendered	30.00
Change	.65

Figure 29: Receipt

Section 8.5.1.1: Transaction Header

A receipt in ARTS contains two major pieces: the header and the body. The transaction header provides a set of entities to describe properties of retail transactions that apply to all components of the transactions (i.e., things that do not vary by transaction line item). These include relationships to customers, currency used in the transaction, and the general entities used to fully describe the transactions, such as the people, place, time, location, and type of business conducted between the store and a party.

Section 8.5.1.2: Transaction Body

When people look at any receipt from a checkout stand, they will see each item is on a separate line. Taxes charged and tender paid are also on their own lines. ARTS has modeled a transaction the same way. The information for each individual item purchased by customers is stored as a separate line item in both POSLog and the ARTS Data Model.

ARTS has identified thirty-three different line item types supported in the transaction body. As one would expect, there are sale and return line items. They can report the taxes paid and the amount tendered with all different kinds of tenders. There is the ability to purchase something for delivery later, and other line items can be taken at the time of checkout. There are line items for managing layaways, rain checks, discounts, rounding, and gift certificates. Customers can pay their utility bills and purchase bread in the same transaction.

Retailers are creative in how they sell their items. This leads to many ways of modifying any and all line items. For example, a discount can apply to the entire transaction, individual items on the transaction, or even a subset of all the items on the transaction.

With thirty-three different line item types, there is extensive support for almost everything that can be done at checkout. There is even extensive support for relating line items in one transaction with line items in other transactions.

Section 8.5.2: Split Transactions

The relationships between transactions can become quite complicated. There can be one transaction that gets split into multiple transactions, and multiple transactions can be merged into one transaction.

One Customer Order Transaction Splits into Multiple Transactions

What happens if customers order something on the web, and part of it gets delivered but the rest is backordered? If retailers wish to recognize the sale, then they create a retail transaction for the tendered and delivered parts, linking them back to the original customer order transaction. Then they create a new customer order transaction for the part of the original customer order transaction for which they have liability, linking it back to the original customer order transaction.

Multiple Customer Order Transactions Get Aggregated into One Transaction

Systems have become so interconnected that the scale in the deli can tell the POS what items customers selected, how much they weigh, and what they cost. The pharmacy can report a prescription sale to the POS. When customers are ready to check out, POS must be able to bring in these transactions from the other departments to take tender for these items, but for reconciliation and loss-prevention purposes, it must link back to the originating transactions.

Section 8.5.3: POSLog—The Lifeblood of Retailing Worldwide

Once the transactional data is entered into the POS, it must be transmitted to other systems in the retail environment. These other systems consume this data.

Transactional data components of POSLog support three major reporting methodologies: the traditional batch end-of-day upload capability, the complete transaction, and the individual components of a transaction. For years, point-of-sale receipt information was kept in a file called a transaction log. When the store closed at the end of the day, this transaction log was transmitted above store using FTP or modems.

When it arrived above store, it was imported into the financial system. From there, many other processes used this information to make decisions around the operation of the store. The import process typically took two days. The first day was used to validate the information, and the second imported it into the database.

As the pace of the world increased, and the Internet became more available, merchandising people needed faster access to sales information. To solve this dilemma, a concept called trickle poll came into being. It allowed each transaction to be sent above store as soon as it was posted to the transaction log.

Today with POSLog, the transaction can be sent up in pieces as soon as each item is added to the order.

Section 8.5.3.1: POSLog Application Interfaces

POSLog is the lifeblood of retail because many of the systems in retail are heavily dependent upon the information contained in POSLog. To start, POSLog is used in accounting to figure out if the store is making a profit. The sales information it contains can be used to update the inventory position. This gives retailers a retail time inventory position. This is very important in today's multichannel sales environment.

Knowing when the replenishment point is reached is imperative to keeping customers happy. Customers do not like going to a store and finding out that what they are looking for is out of stock. Knowing when the replenishment point is reached and how many items are sold during what period helps improve inventory turn rates. Retailers don't want to purchase too much or too little inventory. One costs them money, and the other costs them customers.

POSLog has the ability to track an order from inception to delivery. As discussed when customers start searching on the web and start putting stuff in a basket, this first stage is called an order transaction. After a while, customers decide to purchase the items. The transactions moves from being a plain old order to a customer order transaction. The ARTS Data Model takes this and aggregates all related customer order transactions into a customer order. This gives the current state and any changes that occurred along the path. Finally, a customer order gets tendered and delivered; at that point, it becomes a retail transaction. POSLog supports each of these steps.

POSLog information feeds the customer relationship management system to keep track of customers' purchases and any loyalty implications. It also lets retailers know what the customers purchased and helps with any sort of target-marketing campaign.

If retailers offer a layaway option, POSLog can feed this system with the initial purchase, progress payments, and final payments. During the layaway process, retailers maintain a liability to the customers since they have taken their money but not yet given them their items.

For returns management, POSLog can provide guidance on what was returned, how it mapped to the original purchase, and what the disposition is of the returned item. POSLog can be used in the cash office to reconcile the daily tenders and help balance the books.

When customers purchase items that have to be picked up at a warehouse, POSLog can be fed to the warehouse to authorize the warehouse staff to pick the items in preparation for the customers' arrivals. On the receiving side, POSLog can be used to report the arrival of goods at the docks.

If customers order something that needs to be delivered later, such as is typical on a website or for very large items not normally stocked on the showroom floor, POSLog can be used to provide customer delivery information to the warehousing system.

In retail, there are always situations where items disappear. If it is fuel, customers may drive off without paying. Later, they may realize the oversight and come back to pay for the purchase or not. To support this, a write-off line item was introduced. A write-off is a debit item used to reflect retailers' losses in retail transactions where customers take merchandise or use a service without paying for it.

POSLog has a variety of control events that can be used by store management to help safely operate the store. For example, a drawer limit alert can be used to identify when too much money is in the till and some needs to be removed for the safety of the cashier.

If customers want to rent items or purchase serialized items, POSLog has the ability to record the "loaning" of the equipment and any related serial numbers.

What if merchandising wants to figure out what to purchase? POSLog can be used to send summarized or individual sales information to the forecasting engine. If one wishes to summarize sales information and use it to populate the data warehouse, POSLog has this built in.

The POSLog has the capability to not only report what has occurred, but it can be used to send "forecasted" information to other applications. The forecasting system can take the retail transaction data both current and historical, TLD or summary information and turn it into a forecast for future needs. The forecast can then be sent to systems like the merchandising or labor scheduling system via POSLog. Merchandising can compare the "forecast" with current inventory to make purchase decisions. The labor-scheduling system can produce a better schedule based on a variety of associate criteria and projected sales.

Section 8.5.3.2: Shopping Basket for Other Applications

POSLog originally was simply a recording of the sales transaction, but it now provides transactional information and has all the information needed to populate a shopping basket. POSLog has migrated to become the payload wherever we need to provide a shopping basket for evaluation. For example, to price a transaction, one needs the shopping basket. To calculate taxes, one needs the items and any exemptions. To evaluate customer loyalty, one needs the items and customer information. To send information to the kitchen system, one needs the items and any building or cooking instructions. All this information is built into the POSLog schema.

Section 8.6: Transaction Communication (SOA Real-Time, End-of-Day, and Batch Process Models)

Retailers need this POSLog data to make intelligent decisions, pay taxes, and manage loss prevention. Basically, they need this information to profitably operate their stores. How this information gets to them has changed over time. Just like life has accelerated, so to has the pace that this information gets transmitted.

Section 8.6.1: Batch Reporting

For batch reporting, there are several different options contained within the POSLog schema. The first and most granular is the aggregation of all the individual Transaction Level Details (TLD) for every transaction that occurred at the store. The next level of granularity is the summarization of the TLD by item. For example, one store sold fifty-five blue shirts on October 27, 2006, for $250. The lowest level of granularity reports that the store sold $10,000 worth of goods that day. If so desired, the unique component of using XML schemas allows the mixing of each of these levels of granularity in one document.

In a normal enterprise, this summary information has several uses. The first is the normal end-of-day processing. The middle level of granularity gives one support for an extract, transform, load (ETL) capability between the online transaction processing (OLTP) database and the online analytic processing data warehouse (OLAP). Real-time summary-level information can also be used to monitor store performance through a dashboard or alerting environment.

Section 8.6.2: Real-Time Reporting

Because batch processing took two days to get the information to the people who needed it, along came the need for real-time messaging. This allowed these individuals to get their needed information in pieces. It also gave them the ability to respond to changes almost at the drop of a hat.

Real-time reporting led to the need for information at an even faster rate.

Section 8.6.3: POS SOA Services

To really respond to today's customers, information is needed in micro–real time. That is, information is needed as soon as it is entered in the POS. Inventory needs it to make real-time inventory reservations. Customer relationship management needs it to evaluate offers for platinum customers. Managers need it to resolve issues as soon as they arise. In a web environment, this could extend all the way to the supplier to retrieve and report an inventory count on availability to customers.

To support this, POSLog has the capability to send individual line items one at a time as soon as they are entered into the POS. There are three distinct points in the development of a transaction when information can be sent. The first technique is called *On-the-Fly*. In this mode, as each item is entered, the item information is immediately presented to other systems in the store or web.

The second technique is called *One-Behind*. Here, the first item is entered into the POS (or web). When the next item is entered, the first item is made available to other systems in the store. This is one of the major methods used in food service. It allows one to enter an item, make changes, and when one moves to the next item, the first item is made available to start preparation.

The next method is *On-Total*. Here all the items are entered into the POS (web), and when the total key is pushed, the entire list of items is presented to the other systems. Normally, systems that use On-the-Fly or One-Behind send a totaled transaction when they have finished taking in the list of items. For example, a kiosk might use POSLog to take an order to be sent to a checkout counter where customers pay for the items.

Section 8.7: POS Architecture

Section 8.7.1: The POS Architecture Components

The POS has to handle a complicated combination of business activities that include identifying merchandise and services, calculating the retail price, calculating taxes, collecting and verifying tender, and collecting customer information, including loyalty program parameters and settlement.

Once the activities that POS must perform are identified, one can look at the components of POS needed to accomplish those activities.

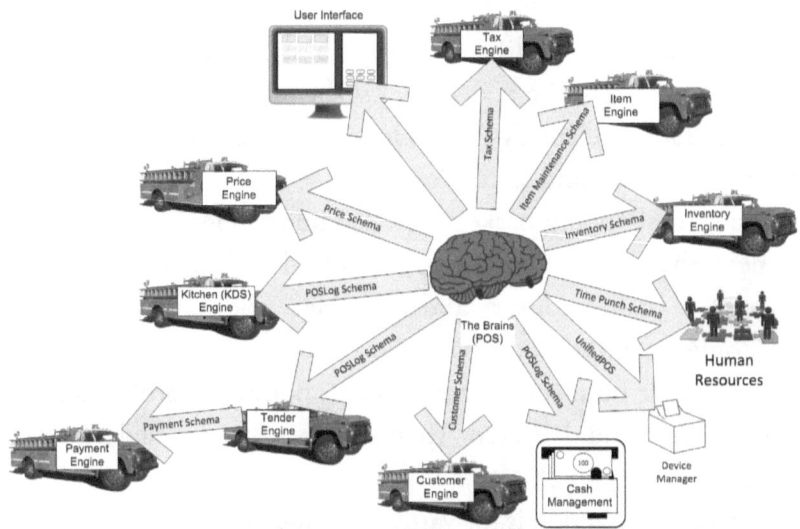

Figure 30: The POS

The POS typically contains a number of "engines" to help it control and process the sales process. The first of these is the device manager from which all the devices are controlled. When a customer's order transaction begins, an item is scanned. The scanner returns a scan code to the POS for it to interpret. The POS sends this off to the second engine, the item engine. There, the item is identified, and any pertinent information is returned.

Depending on the item, the POS may go to the inventory engine to determine the inventory position for the item. Assuming the item is in stock and available, the POS then directs the item, and possibly a shopping basket, to the price engine. In a simple POS, the price engines calculate the prices for the items and/or the shopping basket. The prices are returned to the POS. While this is going on, the customers are asked to swipe their loyalty cards through the magnetic stripe reader (MSR).

When all the items are scanned and priced out, the POS sends the shopping basket (along with any customer information) to the loyalty engine. There, the customers are identified and points are added to their loyalty accounts (or specific programs). It's possible that one or more of the items will be paid for with points from the customers' loyalty accounts. The modified shopping basket is returned to the POS where it is directed to the tax engine. If the retailers are in Europe, the tax calculation is relatively easy. However, in the United States, tax calculations can be quite complicated.

When the shopping basket is totaled and tender is requested from customers, the payment engine gets involved and in conjunction with the device manager collects and authorizes the tender provided by the customers. The operator bags the customers' items. The customer leaves with their purchases in tow. At this point, the order transaction is both tendered and delivered. Therefore, it is transformed into a retail transaction.

The retail transaction is forwarded to almost all the other systems in the retail environment. The financial accounting system gets updated. The inventory management system decrements the inventory position for the items in the retail transaction.

Section 8.7.1.1: The Brains (The POS)

A POS is the brains behind the operation of all the engines. It choreographs the engines to achieve the desired result of selling something to customers and recording the cash taken in. To accomplish this goal, it interfaces with a host of engines, each an expert in its own right.

That sounds simple, but it is way more complicated because it has to asynchronously interface to each engine while keeping the entire receipt intact. For example, while operators are scanning items, customers may swipe their loyalty cards. Although entered at this point in time, the items to which it could apply may not yet have been scanned.

Section 8.7.1.2: The User Interface

Easy to use is easy to say, but very hard to implement. It must start with understanding the business processes that drive the application. Then it takes into account the priorities for each step in the process and optimizes against those priorities. With today's tools, anyone can put together a user interface. The challenge is to create one that makes the business money and keeps customers coming back.

The user interface must be designed to get customers through the checkout process quickly and accurately. There are a number of other standards around the user interface, so ARTS has not tried to create any standards in this area.

Section 8.7.1.2.1: In Retail

Originally, the operator interface was a key component of the selling process. In those times, the operator would manually enter the items. However, with the advent of scanning, the user interface has become more of a confirmation that the items were entered correctly and correcting problems.

Section 8.7.1.2.2: In Food Service

The opposite is true in food service. This user interface is the primary method for inputting customers' choices. Therefore, the menu layout is critical to quickly and correctly enter these items. The more efficient the layout of the menu, the quicker the operator can serve one customer and then help the next, resulting in a faster speed of service. Speed of service is a key performance measure in food service.

Section 8.7.1.3: The Tax Engine

Retailers sell things in as many different ways as they can come up with. To support this, the ARTS Data Model addresses sales tax issues (based on the origin and/or destination of the order), split shipments (one order with different line items shipped to different addresses), different payment options, and different suppliers. On top of that, taxes can be charged against the entire transaction and/or individual items in the transaction. Various tax exemptions can also be made against the entire transaction and/or individual items in the transaction.

ARTS XML Transaction Tax Technical Specification V2.0.0

The two-volume, 228-page specification was released in December 2008. It was developed by twenty-two individuals representing seventeen different companies. It covered two aspects of calculating taxes. The first aspect was keeping up with all the tax changes. To do this, retailers need to regularly update the tax engine with all the new tax rules. The second aspect deals with every transaction; retailers need to calculate the correct tax due by applying the appropriate tax rules. Version two was fully SOA enabled to allow the ability to look up taxes based on a variety of different criteria, such as jurisdiction, taxable group, customer, or much more complicated tasks, such as looking up taxes based on one or more rules.

Tax Discussion

ARTS supports the following model for tax reporting, starting with the location where the taxes are collected. This location is called a situs. A situs is located within a region. This region is where all the various kinds of taxes for this situs are the same. Within a region, there are multiple tax jurisdictions. Each jurisdiction can impose its own taxes on the region. For example, there can be a school situs. The region where the school is location may be within a city. The city is located in a county, and the county is located within a state. Each of them is its own jurisdiction; the school district, the city, the county, and the state have their own tax implications on the region around the school. It becomes very complicated for each jurisdiction to collect its own taxes. So this is left to a tax authority. The tax authority collects all the taxes, and then it distributes to each jurisdiction its taxes.

In the United States, most taxes are defined by a tax table, with the change in the tax being dependent on the total price of the shopping basket. Of course, if real life was only that simple. There are all kinds of tax rules that modify the simple tax table. The ARTS Data Model has the ability to store all these various complicated taxation rules.

As you would expect, the tax rules view defines what is taxable, when it is taxable, where it is taxable, who is liable to pay the tax, and how the tax liability is calculated. The overlapping jurisdiction taxes are likely to be subject to multiple, overlapping sets of taxation rules.

Section 8.7.1.3.1: Tax Maintenance

Because the tax rate is dependent on the situs, it is possible to have a different tax rate at each store. Normally, the enterprise keeps copies of the taxes by site and periodically downloads the data to the site. If there are multiple stores with the same tax rate, they can be grouped together and updated simultaneously.

Section 8.7.1.3.2: Tax-Exempt

Tax-exempt deals with the monetary value of the retail transaction line items that would normally be taxable but are not because of special circumstances. For example, the sale of machinery is normally subject to sales tax. However, when the machinery is used in manufacturing, some taxing jurisdictions consider the sale tax-exempt. A certificate is usually required for an exemption to apply

Tax-exempt status can apply to people. For example, diplomats are tax-exempt. Non-profit organizations also fall into this category.

Section 8.7.1.3.3: Tax Forgiven (Tax Override)

Tax forgiven is very similar to tax-exempt, but it does not require the certificate. It is implicit in the products bought and how they are paid. This is typically things like items bought with food stamps or WIC (Women, Infants, and Children).

With food stamps, the government has developed a list of products that get this treatment; in some cases, it has entered into contracts with particular brands. When customers purchase an item with food stamps, the POS validates the items against the government-approved list. If the items are on the list, it does not charge taxes for those items.

The Tax Engine

A company is not in business to pay taxes, but it must pay taxes to stay in business. Tax is a necessary evil that all businesses must deal with; the smaller you are, the more of your time is consumed with it. This wouldn't be too bad if taxes were constant and consistent all over the place, but unfortunately they shift on the winds of politics and the location of stores.

The primary focus of the taxation for ARTS is calculating and collecting taxes associated with selling, which excludes taxation around asset depreciation or payroll taxes. Basically, sales taxes are collected whenever the ownership of the items changes. ARTS is able to track taxes when items are received by retailers such as a value-added tax (VAT) or when items are sold to the public.

To be able to calculate the various taxes, the ARTS Data Model has the ability to store simple and complex pricing rules. Rules can be applied one at a time or in groups. For example, there is a tax-on-tax model where one tax is applied then added to the item price and a new tax is then calculated on the aggregate.

The ARTS Tax XML Standard has two functions. The first function is to update the tax engine from above store with the latest set of tax rules and amounts. This is necessary in order to perform correct tax calculations. Secondly, the tax engine is used to calculate the tax on the shopping basket being sent from the POS.

These two functions are used to deal with the following tax breakdowns. There are two types of sales taxes covered in ARTS: taxes that are added to the sale at the end of the transaction and taxes that are included in the sales price for each individual item (VAT). To make things easy, there are situations where both a VAT tax and a sales tax are applied to the same item. Taxes can also be additive (tax on tax) as in the case of Canada's GST, HST, and PST set of taxes. There are also situations where taxes are forgiven or exempted.

In addition, there are two points in the transaction where taxes may be applied or not: to the whole transaction amount and/or to individual line items. Normally, taxes on individual items are related to VAT-style taxation. Taxes can be applied to an entire transaction. This is the tradition in the United States where taxes are reported on the bottom of the receipt. These can be mixed. In some jurisdictions, they have to report the taxation on each line item and then summarize it at the bottom of the receipt. This is particularly applicable when some sort of tax exemption or tax forgiven is applied to particular line items in the transaction.

When one applies tax exemptions or overrides, the individual or organization's qualification can be recorded.

The goal of ARTS is not to define taxation that belongs to governments but to provide a place where the tax rules and the results of the application of those rules can be transmitted and stored.

Taxes may be collected at two different points: when the item is sold to customers or when the items are sold to retailers. The ARTS Data Model stores both types of tax collection methods.

Once retailers have collected the taxes, they need to be able to report on it by store, workstation, operator, session, etc. over various reporting period to different jurisdictions.

Section 8.7.1.4: The Item Engine (Item Maintenance)

The item engine is used to find information about an item. For example, an item can be part of a kit. This information will be used by the price engine to calculate the proper price for the item. Or the POS can retrieve and display information about the item to customers.

ARTS Standard Item Maintenance Technical Specification V1.3.0

The 120-page ARTS Item Maintenance Standard V1.3.0 was released at Christmas 2011. Exchanging items for money is the fundamental requirement for retail. This standard allows retailers to look up information about items in a wide variety of different and complex criteria. It covers looking up simple items, kits (combos in food service), making things available during different time periods, being able to display item information on displays throughout the enterprise, transforming items from bulk to sellable items, and all variations of returns, such as how to dispose of returned items (return to vendor, return to shelf, etc.).

Item Maintenance Discussion

The item is the baseline element of retail; a retail enterprise exists to make a profit by selling items. Ideally, there is only one system that "owns" the item file or list of items the enterprise sells. However, for a number of different reasons, there are typically several different systems of record for the item file. Companies buy other companies and inherit their item files. In some cases, it is their business model to have different concepts with item files optimized for the particular business. In order to properly run the business, the people at the enterprise level need to aggregate these into one version of the truth.

Many systems in the enterprise depend on item information. The closer one is able to get to this single version of the truth, the better it is for everyone.

In ARTS, an item is either a physical product or a service. If the item is in inventory, it can be sold, and the sales are tracked. Each item has some sort of unique identifier called an Item ID. As noted earlier, an Item ID can be a SKU, a GTIN, a UPC, etc.

There is a difference between an item and an inventory of items. Sometimes people mistake or misname an item file to confuse it with the inventory file. Basically an item is a description around a particular product, i.e., large blue shirt. It contains rules around selling the item, i.e., can't sell alcohol to minors. Whereas an inventory is a position statement around how many items are in the store and where they are located. As such, it is easy to confuse the two.

Item maintenance originally was a vehicle for populating the item file. But during the process of creating the standard, it became clear that there needed to be a way for the POS to query the item file. Since the item maintenance already had all the elements and attributes, it was a natural extension to enable a POS to inquire the item file to retrieve and verify item information.

The item-maintenance schema is used to update the item files used by the POS to retrieve a wide variety of information about an item. To uniquely identify all kinds of item information, there are over 150 attributes and elements in this schema. This information can be used to make decisions about the proper selling of the item.

ARTS worked closely with GS1 when creating this schema. There were many reasons for this. First ARTS tries not to create a standard where one exists. Also ARTS wants to use the same names where they already exist. It doesn't make any sense to have two standards or two terms for the same thing. Now retailers can track items from the supplier through the warehouse to the shelf and into customers' cars.

An interesting note, some absolute pricing is included in the Item Maintenance XML Standard. This allows one to get the base prices without having to inquire the price engine for things that require no calculations. These include the manufacturer's suggested retail price, the regular sales price, any permanent markdowns, and price levels.

In the item file, there is commonly a set of restrictions. Some of the sales restrictions are so common that ARTS has predefined support for them: age, license, tender type, and sales prohibition. For the age restriction, customers must be over a set age. The license restriction deals with requiring a particular license to purchase a specific item. In some situations only a particular type of tender may be used to purchase certain items, i.e., EBT cannot be used to purchase alcohol. Finally, sales restrictions limit or prohibit the sales during a predefined time period, i.e., no alcohol can be sold before noon on Sunday.

Section 8.7.1.5: The Price Engine (Price)

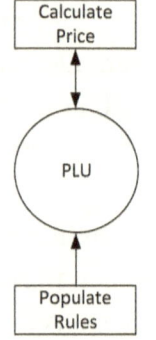

Figure 31: PLU

ARTS Standard XML Price Technical Specification V2.0.1

Price XML Standard V2.01 was released at Christmas 2005 with a partial release of a set of services during Christmas in 2011. There were over twenty individuals representing fifteen different companies involved in creating this ARTS Price XML Standard.

The price schema is designed to supply prices and price rules to populate the price-lookup unit. Then allow different systems to accurately look up prices in a variety of situations, such as looking up the price for a single item, the qualified price tied to some kind of promotion, or the price for an entire shopping basket. The schema allows the price management system to set the prices and rules.

Making sure one has the correct price for an item is critical for a company to make a profit. To this end, pricing goes through its own life cycle. The ARTS Price XML Standard identifies the price at an instance in time. However, prices are dynamic over the life of the item, and this information is stored in the ARTS Data Model.

One can use this history to evaluate the overall effectiveness of the pricing model by comparing the price changes against sales. Retailers modify the model for any item to try to maximize sales and profits. By aggregating the price models for all items in a department, retailers can determine the overall effectiveness of each department. If foot traffic patterns from video analytics are brought into the mix, the effectiveness of the entire store layout can be evaluated. One can even correlate changes in traffic patterns to various promotions. Promotions are there to bring consumers into the store. Now the impact on traffic patterns can be fully understood.

When some sort of promotion is created to help drive sales, a real-time price calculation becomes necessary to properly sell the item. To look up the simple price for an item is quite trivial. However, retailers are quite creative in enticing customers into their stores with various promotions. This drives the need for a complex pricing engine. On top of that, items are sold through many channels. This drives a need for consistent pricing—no matter what channel the customers use.

Consistent pricing can be accomplished by keeping all the price lookup units synchronized. If the number of stores is small and located close to each other, this is manageable. However, growing the number and locations of stores throws in a lot of different channels, and keeping everything synchronized is almost impossible.

A single pricing engine is the best way to support consistent pricing. In the past, this was difficult to do. Basically, the infrastructure wasn't there. However, today it is quite possible to have a single copy of the pricing engine in the cloud so everyone can access it. Several companies have done this and describe the latency issue as a non-starter. The cloud environment has performed so well that there has not been any noticeable slowdown in the checkout process.

Section 8.7.1.5.1: How Is an Item Priced?

When a new product is introduced retailers must figure out what to charge. Once retailers can identify the items they are selling, they need to figure how much to charge for the items. There are many models for determining pricing. Each retailer uses the method that seems appropriate for them. The key area for ARTS is the ability to communicate and record the results of those various calculations.

The most important piece is the cost of the items. The ARTS Data Model supports a variety the basic costs, such as the base cost, the landed cost, and the net cost. On top of the cost of goods comes the handling costs associated with moving the items

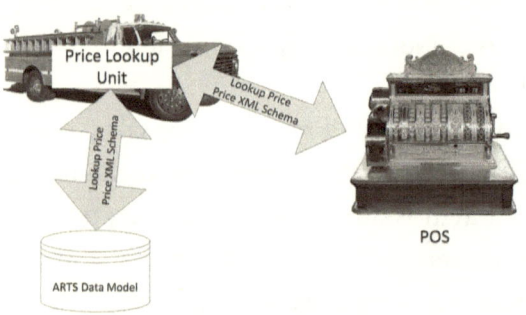

Figure 32: Price Lookup

Prices are set for particular items in at least two ways. The first is fixed pricing. Most items in a store are fixed-price. At the simplest level, they take how much it cost them to purchase the item, add in their cost to sell the item, and finally add in how much profit they wish to make. There are many different ways to calculate this, and there are many different components to each calculation. Those calculations will be left to the accountants. The price becomes the regular sales price for the item.

The second method is price derivation. In price derivation, some rules are put into place to determine the price. These can vary by transaction.

Price rules consist of two components. The first component defines the criteria that must be satisfied by a transaction to trigger the application of a price-derivation rule. In the ARTS Data Model, this is referred to as an eligibility rule. The second component is the actual rule for modifying the base retail price retrieved during price lookup from the price file.

In one sense, these price rules are dependent upon what is purchased, who has purchased it, when was it purchased, and where was it purchased. Any of these can be dependent or independent variables in the pricing equation. The merchandising group takes a variety of inputs from things such as POSLog, the business goals, and objectives to plan the price life cycle. At times, the price is the regular sale price. At other times, the organization decides to run a promotion to improve sales. During the period of the promotion, the price is reduced, which is called the promotional price. A sale results in a temporary price change to the item. At the end of the sale, the price returns to the regular sales price. This pattern may be repeated many times during the life of the item.

Finally, when the item reaches the end of its life, say a swimsuit in September, they start marking down the price to sell the remaining items. In an ideal situation, one markdown clears out the remaining inventory. That makes determining the correct markdown price important to maximize the store's profit while eliminating inventory. This is simple pricing; things become much more complicated when kit pricing comes into play or when loyalty/target marketing is added. To summarize, there is the regular sales price, the promotional price, and the markdown price.

Pricing calculations can be complex. For example, multiple price derivations can be calculated concurrently on a single item or group of items or they may follow in a particular order. Also, pricing rules are typically tied to a marketing calendar and have both a beginning and an ending date, for example, the Christmas season or St. Patrick's Day.

When the sale is completed, one not only wants to record the price of the item being sold was but also what triggered any price change (senior citizens' day, a birthday, 10 Percent Tuesday, etc.). In the POSLog transaction, there is a place to record whatever price rule was used.

In some places, the law requires retailers to give the best price it can to their customer. To do this, the PLU must implement what is called the best-pricing algorithm. In other words, if the operator rings up the items in a kit (combo for food service) separately, the PLU must figure this out and charge the reduced combo price.

Another common pricing algorithm is called mix-and-match. This is when retailers have a box of items from which customers may select anything in the box. The PLU must identify if the correct number of the right kinds of qualified items are scanned before calculating the mix-and-match price for the selection.

Beyond the legal requirements, customer loyalty comes into play. For example, if there is targeted marketing, the PLU must take that into account. Once customers are identified, that information needs to be fed to the loyalty system where the associated promotion is validated. That validation needs to be fed to the PLU where it can be used to modify the price of any associated item.

If retailers are running a promotion, there has to be an interface with the merchandising system to get the latest promotions and rules.

Having the ability to get the same price for an item—no matter the shopping channel—is an enormous value to consumers. Customers don't like seeing one price on the shelf label only to find a higher price at the checkout stand. Having a schema that works across a variety of infrastructures helps provide the consistency consumers desire.

Another use is for shelf labels. In some places, if the price on the shelf is different from the price engine, retailers must charge the lower price. Having this information saved in the ARTS Data Model helps provide consistent pricing across channels (POS, web, and mobile).

ARTS Price Life Cycle Optimization RFP

On December 25, 2005 ARTS released the ARTS Price Life Cycle Optimization Request for Proposal. This RFP helped select the right pricing solution for businesses. It followed price throughout its life cycle from a new item price through final clearance pricing. It included the functionality needed for pricing promotions, markdowns, optimization, and demand forecasting.

The tabs dealt with creating and managing master data for use in an SOA environment. It deals with the regular sale price, and then it changes to that price. If the price change is temporary, then it is a promotion. At the end of the promotion period, the price is returned to the regular sale price. At the end of the season, the price is permanently reduced to eliminate the remaining inventory. This permanent price change is called a markdown. It is also possible, however rare, to permanently increase the price, and this is called a markup. The RFP also has tabs on price optimization, decision support, analytics, and demand forecasting to help figure out what price should be charged.

Item Price Maintenance

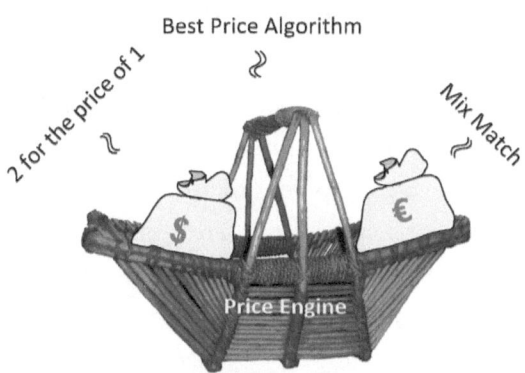

Figure 33: Price Calculations

During the life of an item, most of the item information remains constant with the exception of its price and location. Price changes and price derivation rule changes are the most frequent types of maintenance performed on retailers' items and price files. Typically, most item and retail price maintenance is planned and centrally directed from the home office. A business unit may initiate limited price changes to correct errors or deal with a local competitive situation on an exception basis.

Changes typically involve three areas. New items are added or existing descriptions are changed in response to some marketing plan. Prices can also be changed according to the life cycle. These are typically permanent price changes, such as markdowns or markups.

They permanently change the price on all items in inventory, or price rules are changed in response to some marketing plan.

Section 8.7.1.6: The Inventory Engine (Inventory)

ARTS XML Inventory Technical Specification V2.1.0

ARTS released V2.1 of the Inventory XML Standard on Christmas of 2011. The team involved twenty-six members from seven different retailers and nineteen vendors.

Inventory, in its most basic form, is a simple list of all the things retailers have in their stores. In reality, there is a lot more; of those items in stock, retailers need to know how many items are available for sale, where those items exist, the state of those items, when they can be sold, and who can sell them. In a multichannel environment, customers want to know where the items they are looking for exist, how much they cost, and how quickly they can get one. Ideally, the inventory management system knows what retailers have and where things are located.

Inventory is one of the largest cost centers that retailers have to deal with. It requires constant monitoring to make sure there is enough stock at the right location to satisfy customers. Or to say it another way, they must have enough stock to turn consumers into customers.

Section 8.7.1.6.1: Store Inventory Management

Inventory keeps a running total of the items in each location. Every time an item is sold, transferred, or returned, the current inventory position for that item at that location gets adjusted. Items get moved, broken, or stolen, and the inventory has to be counted periodically.

In a traditional enterprise, items are received from trucks or trains at the loading docks of the distribution center. They are either cross-docked or put into storage in bins, on shelves, etc. From the distribution center, the items are shipped to the store and usually put on shelves. Once on the shelves, they are sold to, stolen by, or moved by customers.

To get an accurate measure they need to be counted periodically and compared to the count in the inventory management system

There are two types of inventory counts. There is a physical count that counts every item in inventory. As one can surmise, this is a very labor- and time-intensive exercise. As such, it is only done periodically. The other type of inventory count is called a cycle count. Cycle counts are also performed periodically; however, only a selected group of items are counted. Some of them are selected randomly; others are chosen based on things like inventory turn.

A physical count is normally done once a year for tax purposes. A cycle count is normally done four times a year with random sampling done in-between. Once the count is complete, the information is fed into the inventory management system and sent to accounting.

In today's multichannel world, there is a new view of inventory. This is the direct-to-consumer model. In this model, customers order the items from retailers, but they are shipped directly to customers from the suppliers or vendors.

One of the inputs to the inventory management system is POSLog, the output of the point of sale. It records what items where sold and when. Whenever an item is sold or returned or ordered for later delivery or pickup, the inventory position and/or state have to be updated. In addition, if it is return, the disposition must be added. Basically, the returned item needs to be sent back to the supplier, put back on the shelf (updating the quantity on hand), or be disposed.

The stock on hand is updated for every sale; when it reaches a predefined restocking point, the inventory is automatically reordered.

Stock that is part of a seasonal plan is ordered in preparation for the season. When the season starts, this stock's inventory state changes to make it available to sell.

Section 8.7.1.6.2: Customer Inventory Management

The other side of inventory management deals with customers. These customers are looking for a particular item. They can either order things online or through a catalogue. They can check the availability of particular items. If the item is available, much like the store reservation, customers can order the item and create an inventory reservation on their purchases. If they are in the store and the item is not on the shelf or it is the wrong size or color, they can order it. This creates an inventory reservation for the item, which ties it to this particular customer. In today's world, customers can go online and watch the various stages of the delivery for their items. When the item arrives at the store, the customer can be notified.

When customers have finished the order process and paid for their purchases, the information gets recorded in POSLog as a customer order transaction, which further translates into an ARTS Data Model customer order. The information is sent on through to the ARTS Data Model inventory view to record the change in the status of the items.

What's cool is that the items can be stocked by the supplier and shipped directly to consumers without going through the store's distribution center, reducing costs.

Section 8.7.1.6.3: Inventory Management

Each of these inventory states needs to be stored and managed. The ARTS Data Model saves all of this data in the various inventory and stock ledger views.

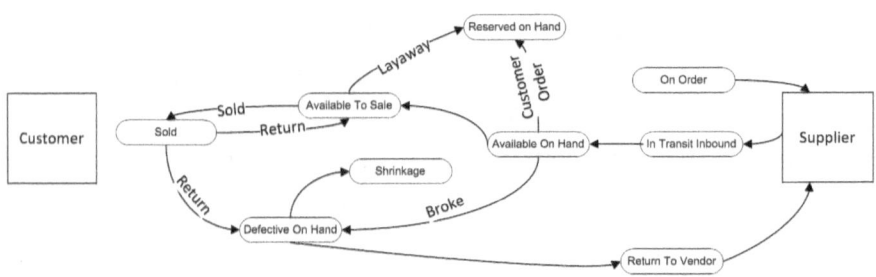

Figure 34: Inventory State Diagram

- *in transit inbound*—items must be in the store in order to sell them. Items leave the vendor/supplier and become "in transit inbound."
- *available on hand*—when they arrive in the store, they update inventory and become "available on hand." The retailer may not want to put them on the floor because they are waiting for a promotion, like a back-to-school sale.
- *available to sale*—stock moves from available on hand to "available to sale" when the selling criterion is met. The stock is now ready for customers to purchase.
- *sold*—once a customer purchases an item, its inventory state moves to "sold." The inventory count for this item is decremented, and when a restocking point is reached, it can be reordered.
- *on order*—if customers or retailers order an item, the state of the order becomes "on order."
- *reserved on hand*—if customers special order an item, retailers can mark it as "reserved on hand." This will save this stock for the customer who ordered it.
- *shrinkage*—periodically stock is counted. A physical count is done when retailers want to count every item in stock. This is typically done for tax purposes. Another type of counting is called a cycle count. This only counts some of the items in the store, typically the most desirable from a loss-prevention perspective. When either count is done, the difference between what is listed in inventory and the actual count is listed as "shrinkage." With this information, an alarm can occur.

When a customer returns an item, the item goes in one of three different directions. If the item is fixable, it goes to the vendor who supplied the retailer with the item. This is a "Return to Vendor" state. If, on the other hand, it can be repaired locally, it becomes "Defective on Hand." If neither one, then the item is "Shrinkage," basically thrown away.

Section 8.7.1.6.4: Item Inventory and Stock Ledger

The ARTS Data Model maintains the financial and inventory balances for items carried in the enterprise. It allows tracking inventory by location. That can be complicated since individual items can be in different locations within a single store. At the enterprise level, the number of potential locations expands dramatically. On top of this, one mixes in items that are too big to be stored locally and must be shipped from the vendor. Next, throw in Internet or catalogue sales, and inventory management gets quite complicated.

All of this management is important because retailers want to keep their customers happy by being able to sell them things no matter where the items are physically located. This has led to the need for retailers to be able to check for items in inventory in other stores, to be able to reserve the item in that other store for a particular customer, and to direct customers to the other store or have the item shipped to the customer.

Think about the accounting problem. The item is in store B's inventory, but the transaction occurred in store A. If you are a store manager, do you get credit for the sale? When you restock, do you restock both stores? What if it is a slow-moving item? To simplify this, it is not uncommon for a transfer of ownership of the inventory for that item from store B to store A.

There must be messages communicating all this activity and places to store the results. The ARTS Inventory XML Standard communicates all the inventory positions and movement, and the ARTS POSLog reports the sale. The ARTS Data Model is the place to store the actions and keep the running totals.

Section 8.7.1.6.5: Item Inventory—Selling

Items leave a store in a number of different ways. The most common way is being sold to customers. This is what retail is all about, exchanging goods and services for tender. The next way items leave the store is by being given to customers. This can be done either through a promotion or through a gift certificate. These first two methods are reported with a POSLog message.

The next way items leave the store is through theft. Outside of security techniques that catch criminals in action, the result of the theft shows up during an inventory count (physical or cycle). The last way items leave the store is through breakage. Either of these methods is in an inventory message.

No matter how an item leaves the store, the removal from its inventory position must be decremented so that the inventory can be reordered when replenishment levels are reached. This becomes important when the inventory for an item reaches a replenishment level for one location, but another location has an excess of the same item. A stock transfer can be initiated to move the stock from the location with an excess inventory to the location needing replenishment. Stock transfers are reported with the inventory message.

Of course, nothing is really that simple. To decide if one location has an excess of inventory, one must examine inventory turn rates. If there are more items than can be sold, based on inventory turn rates, then that location has an excess inventory. Inventory turn rates are a key performance indicator (KPI) derived from the information contained in the ARTS Data Warehouse.

Section 8.7.1.6.6: Warehouse Management RFP

A key component of inventory is the distribution center. To help retailers purchase a warehouse management product, in May of 2005, ARTS created a Warehouse Management RFP.

The Warehouse Management RFP Excel spreadsheet has seventeen tabs covering features and functions for everything from the truck arriving and being sent to a location in the yard or to a dock to managing put-a-way or cross-docking. It covers quality assurance inspections, including vendor analysis. On the shipping side, it talks about wave management for picking and packing. It covers replenishment and returns management. Throughout the entire process, it updates inventory to show its current state.

Section 8.7.1.7: The Tender Engine (POSLog)

A long time ago, customers paid for their purchases by exchanging an item, such as a chicken, they brought in to trade. Then money was invented to make the trading easier. Instead of bringing a chicken to trade for milk, customers only had to bring the cash equivalent. Customers in the American West would only have cash when they harvested their crops. This meant they couldn't buy things between harvests. Retailers started giving them credit to tie them over between crops. From there, the number of tendering options has significantly grown. Today's POSs tender engines have to handle virtually any way customers wish to pay—except for paying with chickens.

ARTS provides robust support for a large number of these different tenders. In addition to traditional tender media like cash, checks, credit cards, and debit cards, ARTS supports a wide variety of vouchers like coupons, food stamps, gift certificates, customer trade accounts, etc. In addition, it supports the new smart card technology, and the mobile model. There is special support for Europay MasterCard and Visa (EMV) standard. One can tender to a store account or use loyalty points for tendering.

Section 8.7.1.7.1: Retail Transaction—Tender—Coupon

What is a coupon? In its fundamental form, it is a reduction in the price of an item by a predefined amount to entice a customer to purchase something. That amount is printed on the coupon. It is either a fixed amount or a percentage off. To redeem a coupon, customers must purchase the item or brand identified on the coupon.

There are two ways coupons are handled in ARTS. If a coupon is a manufacturer's coupon, then it is tendered after taxes are applied. The other type of coupon is a store coupon. This type of coupon is considered a promotion. As such, it is applied prior to calculating the taxes.

Manufacturer's coupons are paid for by the manufacturer; as such, they set the amount of the discount. Manufacturer coupons are not a discount, which reduces the price of the item. In effect, they are another tender type. Typically, at the end of day after reconciliation, they are collected from all the tills and sent off to companies who separate the coupons by manufacturer. The collections are shipped to the manufacturer for redemption. In today's world, this can be done electronically

Here's an interesting twist: if retailers have a double coupon day special and customers use a manufacturer's coupon, one of the coupon redemptions is applied after taxes are calculated and used as tender. However, the coupon double is considered a promotion and applied prior to taxes being calculated.

Taxes are a tricky subject and are unique in every jurisdiction. ARTS provides places to transmit and store tax information, but tax authorities all over the world define the content.

Section 8.7.1.7.2: Retail Transaction—Tender—Authorization

Each type of tender requires a different level of authorization before retailers accept it to settle customer purchases. In part, the authorization level is a function of the fraud or default risk associated with each tender type. In the United States, cashiers use a special pen on $20 bills to validate the bill is made of the proper materials.

Floor and ceiling limits may be placed on different types tender. For example, stores often impose minimum purchase amounts on credit card charges. Of course, there has always been the need to authorize credit and debit card transactions. In Europe, Europay MasterCard Visa (EMV) also requires authorization. On top of this, smart cards and PINs have to be verified.

Section 8.7.1.7.3: Retail Transaction— Tender—Account View

One of the first kinds of non-cash tender was customer accounts. Retailers would let their customers "borrow" to pay for their purchases by entering the amount owed into a book. The customer would pay at some predefined time like when they sold their herd or sold their wheat or got paid. This type of account is still used today but with a little more rigor. In addition, today retailers have their own credit cards for in-store purchases. ARTS has the ability to transmit and store the supporting information.

Businesses can also use these store accounts to purchase items for use in their business; an example is purchasing pencils and paper. One unique aspect is the number of authorized purchasers can be a lot more than in a family. On top of this, many times the person picking up the items is not the person authorized to purchase the items. A purchase order is signed by the authorized agent and used by the store to deliver the items.

There is a special type of account used originally by the trucking industry to allow truckers to purchase food, fuel, and lodging—but not other kinds of items. These are called fleet cards. Today, other variations of this concept are used by the United States federal government to help women, infants, and children (WIC). This program has become so sophisticated that the government will work out deals with particular vendors to only allow purchases of that vendor's products. For example, instead of being able to buy any kind of cereal with WIC, consumers are only able to purchase one brand.

These variations all need the ability to authorize the person making the purchase. Just as with a credit card, the ARTS Data Model provides support for storing the authorization information.

Section 8.7.1.7.4: Voucher

In one sense, everything used for tender is a voucher. Even cash is a form of voucher. In ARTS, it is defined as any instrument that has some stored monetary value. For example, customers purchase vouchers, such as for a car wash, and retailers need to record this sale as a line item. Vouchers may need to record a unique voucher number, which can be used as a redemption code.

Think about how a car wash purchase is redeemed. The customer purchases the car wash during the fueling process. He or she then drives to the car wash bay to enter the redemption code for the car wash. If the car wash is not working or customers need to delay redemption, they will come back later to redeem. Because of the delay between purchase and redemption, retailers have a financial liability during this time. Basically, retailers have money that is not yet theirs. To limit their liability, many will put an expiration date after which the money's ownership transfers to retailers. Why would this happen? Normally customers either forget they purchased the car wash or they lose the receipt.

Another way to reduce retailer liability is for retailers to charge a fee to maintain these accounts. Eventually, these fees can erode the original amount to the point there isn't any equity left. This has the same effect as an expiration date.

Section 8.7.1.7.5: Stored Value

ARTS IXRetail Stored Value Technical Specification V1.0.0

On June 4, 2003, ARTS released the first version of the Stored Value XML Standard. There were twelve different companies that created this standard. This was of ARTS's first XML Standards. There were eleven use cases used in the design of this Standard.

Stored Value Discussion

ARTS uses the term stored value to refer to a whole class of payment options where the money is given to retailers up front and used to pay for purchases at a later time. The customer accesses the money through some sort of instrument, such as a certificate or a card. The retailers maintain financial liability until customers use the instrument to redeem for goods or services.

Figure 35: Stored Value

There is a whole set of processes associated with stored value instruments. First, they must be set up and tender is added; tender is removed during the purchase process, and individuals can be added to the account. Periodically, individuals wish to inquire about the amount of money on the instrument; at some point, money gets added to the instrument, and at the end of its life, people need to be able to close out the instrument.

Stored Value Types:

- *cash/gift cards*—cash and gift cards can have their balances increased (be "charged") with money value and may or may not allow the balance to be increased again (be "recharged"). These cards are used as tender in sales transactions, causing their balances to be decreased.
- *store credits*—value is stored as a credit that can only be redeemed for merchandise within retailers' store chains. Cash will not be given back. It is identified usually by a unique number associated with customers, which is used as a key to look up the cash value in the store's database.
- *gift certificates*—one-shot use and any difference between the value and items purchased is refunded in cash, a new gift

certificate is issued with a value equal to the remaining balance, or they lose it!

- *phone cards*—phone cards issued by retailers can have a dual role in that any monetary value stored on the card can be used as tender with the amount of tender being decremented from the value stored.

- *loyalty points*—point accumulation and redemption for customer loyalty programs can be transacted using stored value messages.

For years, the payment arena had changed little. Customers paid with cash, check, credit, or debit. The credit card companies and the banks owned the payment side. With mobile contactless, and mobile wallets, payment technology has become very dynamic with new players changing the payment landscape.

To support the changing landscape, ARTS has moved to support pushing the payment engine into its own box. Now as things change, retailers only need to replace/upgrade this isolated payment engine. One of the benefits is the ability to segregate the entire payment world from all the rest of retailers' infrastructure. In a world where hackers abound, this small footprint can be secured and audited for PCI-DSS, chip, and PIN/EMV regulations. In addition, the smaller system envelope means reduced certification costs.

Tendering is another complicated engine in the POS. Besides being able to take in a wide variety of tender types, the POS must guarantee the privacy of the customers' information. This is the key area where the payment card industry (PCI) standard gets involved. The PCI standard provides guidance around securing credit card information and fines with penalties if this information gets compromised.

ARTS XML Payments Integration White Paper V2.0.0

The PCI standard has put an enormous burden on the retail industry to protect customer credit card numbers. This requires extensive auditing and monitoring everywhere the credit card numbers could be stored.

The solution is to isolate exposure to the credit card numbers to as small a footprint as possible. ARTS started working on a set of use cases to isolate the payment process from the rest of the retail infrastructure. This would put the box around the payment processing.

ARTS discovered some surprises when building its use cases. Over time, banks, acquirers, and retailers came across the idea of mixing customer loyalty systems with credit cards. The idea was to offer customers loyalty points if they used the branded credit card. This way, customers got points, retailers made money on the sale, and the acquirer network made money on the use of the credit card. The kink in the deal occurs was when one tries to secure the credit card number by separating the loyalty information. The kink exists because the credit card number evolved into pulling double duty to also be the number for the loyalty system.

The only way to solve this dilemma was to attach the loyalty system to the payment box. The credit card number and the loyalty account were securely isolated from the rest of the retail network. A different problem appeared. Other systems need customer loyalty information to properly include any price reduction to customers or to add loyalty purchases.

Following the philosophy of not creating a standard where one exists, ARTS found an organization in Europe called Electronic Protocols Application Software (EPAS.ORG) that had created a payment integration standard called Sale-to-POI Integration Standard. The interesting part is that they were primarily staffed by acquirers and banks. On the other side of the payment process, ARTS is staffed by retailers and vendor, the opposite side of the same pipeline. Since the schema existed, by leveraging ARTS knowledge, ARTS helped extend it to properly support retail and align version 1.0 with ARTS's names. ARTS then developed a set of use cases to show how to use the EPAS. ORG standard.

Section 8.7.2: The Kitchen Engine—KDS (POSLog)

Restaurants are considered by many to be mini-factories. In the food-service world, the items sold are typically prepared after they are ordered. To accomplish this, the items ordered by customers are sent to a kitchen where they are displayed on a UnifiedPOS device called a kitchen display system (KDS).

In the KDS, the items are routed to the various stations in the kitchen for processing. The salads are routed to the salad station, the meats are routed to the grill, and the desserts are routed to the dessert bar. The kitchen display system is used to show the order to the appropriate cook and manages all the various customer orders on this remote order display.

Each display is divided into areas representing each customer's order. When the order is finished and delivered to the customer, the cook pushes a button on another UnifiedPOS Device called the bump bar to notify the waiter that the order is ready and to move the order off the screen.

Section 8.7.3: Device Manager (UnifiedPOS)

The kitchen display subsystem leads to a discussion around all the devices connected to the POS.

ARTS UnifiedPOS Technical Specification V1.14.0

When people buy a mouse for a laptop, they expect to be able to plug the mouse into the laptop and just have it work. This works because of a standardized definition for the interface to the mouse. ARTS has created standardized interface definitions for thirty-six devices that can be physically attached to a POS. It starts with the scanner working through the credit card magnetic stripe reader to the cash drawer to the receipt printer and everything in between.

This standard, called UnifiedPOS, is ARTS most adopted standard with almost universal adoption by all the major device vendors. The interface definition is called an application-programming interface (API). An API is the definition of the interface for accessing the properties, methods, and events for the device. A property might be the font used for the printer. The methods used by the device to accomplish something might be telling the printer to print a receipt. The events provide unsolicited information, such as the printer is out of paper. The combination of these properties, methods, and events make up the definition of the interface to the device. Basically, they tell people how to use the device. There is a separate set of these for each of the thirty-six devices.

Since its inception POS devices have been physically attached to the POS with a wire. Some people took the API definitions in the UnifiedPOS standard and made a driver to interface with the major programming languages used to create POS applications, Java, C++ and C#. These have aided in helping companies properly implement the standard. Part of the reason for UnifiedPOS success is the effort by these people who created these sample implementations.

Anyone who has been to an Apple store has seen the start of the new world for POS systems. The associates use their tablets to help customers find items and checkout. This minimizes the need for customers to stand in long checkout lines. In the mobile world, the wire to these devices needed to be cut. The first iteration of this architecture from UnifiedPOS, leveraged UnifiedPOS version 1.13 used web services and XML to break the connection, called WS-POS. To support this, ARTS ported the property, methods, and events into XML. This porting is called XMLPOS.

There were some limitations to using the first version based on a direct connection in a fully remote environment, for example, being able to dynamically share the device. To fully support different remote connection models, ARTS created UnifiedPOS version two. Some of the capabilities designed into version two include supporting SOA and being able interface between different programming paradigms,

Java and POS for .net. UnifiedPOS version one was a 1990s COM-(component object model) based architecture, and version two is a more modern object-oriented design. The infrastructure should support direct connected devices as in version one but also modern web services and rest architectures. But most important was the ability to automatically and dynamically build a POS by dynamically discovering the needed devices.

Being able to remotely connect to the devices opened up entirely new ways to efficiently use these devices; the dynamic construction was only limited by the imagination. For example, as customers push their carts around the store following the guidance from their store location applications, it leads them from one shelf to the next to find the items on their shopping list. They can fill the cart with their items. An RFID scanner attached to the shopping cart can scan each item as it is put into the cart.

When customers are finished shopping, they can get a total from a virtual POS, including taxes, promotions, etc. They then have several options; one is to pay with their mobile wallets. Another is to go to a payment terminal and pay there. Another is to go to a bank of magnetic stripe readers (MSR) take one, plug it into their mobile phone, and swipe their credit card. They can then go to any printer on the floor and have their receipt printed. Alternatively, they can have a digital receipt sent electronically to their e-mail accounts. On their way out of the store, they can have an associate verify their purchases. Better yet, a video analytics program verifies the purchases in the shopping cart. The only step left is to package the items for delivery to the customers' homes.

Section 8.7.3.1: ARTS UnifiedPOS Device Descriptions

When customers arrive at the checkout stand, they typically put their items on a conveyor belt. The belt moves these items forward to make it easier for the cashier to reach and scan the items. With a scanner, the cashier takes each item, scans the barcode, and places the item in a bag.

While this process is going on, customers can scan their loyalty cards to redeem their rewards or get credit for their purchases.

The next step is for the cashier to total the transaction and collect tender from the customer. The customer can pay for the transaction with cash where the money goes into the till (insert in the cash drawer) or with a credit card or debit card where the card is read with an MSR. The customer can possibly scan the card with a smart card reader. The customer can sign for the purchase on a signature capture device. The POS can print out the receipt on the POS printer and save a copy for the government on the fiscal printer.

The following is a set of brief descriptions of all the devices supported by ARTS UnifiedPOS:

- *belt*—belts are typically located at the checkout stand. The customers put their purchases on the belt, and the operator can programmatically control movement of the belt. UnifiedPOS defines a set of commands for controlling the belt's speed, direction, and start/stop. In addition, it can control add-ons, such as light barriers and security flaps.
- *bill acceptor*—the bill acceptor takes various denominations of cash in various currencies from customers and reports the amount input to the operator. On request, it can report a count of the various quantities in the unit. To keep the device operational, it can report various cash acceptor specific statuses, such as jams, full, near-full, etc. to the operator.
- *bill dispenser*—the opposite of the bill acceptor is the bill dispenser. Here one dispenses a specified amount of cash into a specified exit. To effectively dispense a controlled amount of cash, the dispenser must report its status to the controlling application, including jams and the amount of cash in the device by tender type. One does not want to dispense less cash than the customers expect. One could take money into the bill acceptor, calculate the appropriate change, and then use the bill dispenser to return the appropriate change to customers.

- *biometrics*—biometric devices capture biometric information used to verify or identify individuals. Biometric data is almost impossible to duplicate from one individual to the next; for example, everyone's fingerprints are unique. The biometric device must be able to allow customers to enroll by capturing their biometric data. Then when customers want to be validated, the biometrics device must capture customers' data so that it can be verified. An interesting observation is that the initial capture requires higher-quality data than the verification does. The device allows for the configuration of an acceptance tolerance. If the two measurements are within the acceptable tolerance, we have a match.

- *bump bar*—the bump bar is used in the kitchen of a food-service establishment to manage customer orders. It is used in conjunction with a remote order display (ROD). The ROD is divided into areas. Each area is loaded with an individual customer order and associated with a button on the bump bar. After the order is prepared, the corresponding button on the bump bar is pressed to tell the kitchen display system that this order is finished, can be delivered to customers, and should be removed from the display.

  The use gets more complicated in a restaurant with multiple stations. One station will be used for making salads, another for cooking meat, and another for preparing deserts.

- *cash changer*—the cash changer takes customers' cash (coins and bills) in and returns the correct change. To meet this objective, the cash changer must keep and be able to report its status on demand. For example, how much cash, in what denominations, and is it jammed. It must also support different currencies when used in an area where different currencies are used, such as an international airport.

- *cash drawer*—the cash drawer is the drawer in the POS where the various tenders are stored and from where change is made. To support the POS, it needs to be open on command from the

POS. Inside the cash drawer, the box where the tender is put is called the till. Tills are retrieved from the cash office at the start of an operator's shift and put into the cash drawer. The till is removed either when the operator takes a break or at the end of a shift, and the till is returned to the cash office for counting.

- *check scanner*—the check scanner is designed to capture the image of a personal or business check. It programmatically controls insertion, reading, and removal of a check. The image can then be stored in its memory for future retrieval. The device can be incorporated with other devices, such as the MICR.

- *coin acceptor*—the coin acceptor device is used to read, sort, count, and store coins. This device is normally found in vending machines. As such, they are stand-alone devices and are able to report their mechanical condition, such as when they are jammed or how many coins are in the device.

- *coin dispenser*—under control of the POS, the coin dispenser releases an application-defined amount of change. As such, the POS needs to know the state of the device. For example, it must know if there is a sufficient amount of change to meet the needs of the POS. Then at the end of the day, it has to be able to support reconciliation. It needs to report current totals as well as transactions that occurred throughout the current period. This device has several uses, such as in a vending machine or a self-checkout position.

- *credit authorization terminal (CAT)*—hackers assault retailers' infrastructure all the time in attempts to get credit card numbers. The credit card companies created PCI in an attempt to force retailers to securely manage their customers' credit card numbers.

  In several places in the world by law, waiters are not allowed to take customers' credit/debit card out of customers' sight. To meet the law, credit authorization terminals (CAT) were created. These portable handheld devices typically consist of a display, keyboard, magnetic stripe card reader, receipt printing device, and a communications device. The CAT terminal effectively shields the POS application and the entire retailer's infrastructure from exposing customers' credit card details from hackers. After all, if the information is not there, no one can steal it.

There is one interesting problem dealing with TIPs (To Insure Promptness). Tips were originally intended as a reward to the server for prompt service. In the United States, politicians saw this as an untapped tax source and started making it a mandatory part of the compensation and tax it accordingly. Recording a tip on a credit card purchase has always been an interesting process. Normally when customers' credit cards are scanned at a food-service establishment, the credit card is authorized for the amount of the transaction plus an extra percentage. Then the transaction is suspended until the actual tip amount is entered, the transaction is finalized, the end-of-day reconciliation occurs, or in twenty-four-hour operations, when the transaction is closed at the end of day and reopened at the start of the next day.

What does this have to do with CATs? Since CATs keep the credit card information locally, CATs have to perform the same set of operations locally. When a transaction is authorized on a CAT, the CAT must communicate to the POS to suspend the transaction until the authorization is finalized.

Since an authorization takes place on a CAT, the reversal must also be processed on the CAT. In addition, a whole set of actions takes place on the CAT that must be communicated to the POS application (everything from the preauthorization, to the authorization completion, to the cancellation).

- *electronic journal*—the electronic journal records and stores a record of the POS receipts. On command, it can reprint specific receipts. When requested, it can transfer these stored POS receipts.
- *electronic value reader/writer*—the electronic value reader/ writer (EVRW) is a new version of the CAT device. It reads

information from customers' contactless or contact IC card containing money, loyalty points, and/or prepaid instruments like vouchers or tickets. The device can perform an electronic settlement on stored value cards.

- *fiscal printer*—in some countries, the law requires the printer to keep a history of all the sales transactions. In addition, there is the need to print out regular receipts and print out slips of paper for the signing of credit card receipts. The ARTS UnifiedPOS fiscal printer handles all three sets of requirements. The journal printer functions keep track of the transactions for the tax authorities. The receipt printer functions print out the regular customer receipts. The slip printer functions are used to print slips of paper for credit card receipts, loyalty information, and promotional offers.

  This is a sample of countries which have legal requirements for fiscal printers: Brazil, Bulgaria, Greece, Hungary, Italy, Poland, Romania, Russia, Turkey, Czech Republic, Ukraine, and Sweden. This is a minimal list; over time, others may be added to this list.

- *gate*—the gate is designed to basically work with a self-checkout station. The gate remains closed during the retail transaction while items are being scanned and the transaction is being tendered. Once the transaction is complete and becomes a retail transaction, notice is given to the gate to open and allow customers to leave.

- *hard totals*—hard totals keeps a set of secure totals files that can temporarily keep transactions in its memory.

- *image scanner*—the image scanner is able to scan an image under command from the host in low-light conditions.

- *item dispenser*—the item dispenser (think vending machines) allows control of dispensing one or more items from multiple slots. As well as reporting the status of the various slots (empty, near-empty, or jammed).

- *key lock*—key lock is simple; devices interface and support reporting position changes for three physical positions (locked, normal, supervisor).
- *lights*—light services are very simple devices. The UnifiedPOS interface to a light allows the light to be turned on and off. It can control multiple lights, blinking lights, and different color lights.
- *line display*—the line display is typically used to keep customers informed during the checkout process. However, they are starting to find uses all over the selling floor. The line display supports both text and graphics type applications. It supports marquee-like scrolling, blinking, and reverse video for highlighting.
- *mag stripe reader*—the magnetic stripe reader (MSR) is the traditional device for reading and writing several standard formats in the magnetic stripe on a credit or debit card. The standard supports reading three tracks used in most of the world (and four tracks in Japan). The standard supports places where drivers' licenses have magnetic stripes. Because security is very important with respect to credit/debit cards, the standard supports encryption and a device to host authentication for detecting and preventing phishing and man-in-the-middle attacks.
- *MICR*—the MICR (magnetic ink character reader) Control is used to read information from a check where the numbers are magnetically encoded on the check following the ANSI MICR standard. It is designed for the POS to control the check-reading process. This is especially important today because many retailers are "cashing" the check immediately during the checkout process.
- *motion sensor*—the motion sensor has the ability to detect and report the presence of someone at the register.
- *pin pad*—the pin pad is used by customers to enter personal identification numbers. For security purposes, the interface supports encrypting PIN information at the device. The

standard describes several PIN pad management systems such as DUKPT.

- *point card*—the point card reader/writer is a plastic card similar to a credit card where tender information can be stored and redeemed. The device needs to be able to read and write changes to the card in a variety of different formats. It also has the ability to print.

- *POS keyboard*—the POS keyboard reads the keys from the entire or a subset of the POS keyboard.

- *POS power*—the power device provides a standardized POS unique interface to a UPS (Uninterruptable Power Supply). It provides support to shutdown, restart, or suspend the UPS. It has the ability to inform the application about the state of the power as well as the state of the UPS system. UnifiedPOS has traditionally been an exclusive-use model. That is, each device can be used by only one application at a time. However, POS power is explicitly defined as a shareable device. This means that multiple applications can access the properties, and methods can be shared.

- *POS printer*—there are three generic uses for the POS printer: as a receipt printer, as a slip printer to print one line to sign for credit card purchases, and as a journal printer to print transaction history.

- *remote order display*—the remote order display is a type of video unit typically used in a kitchen to provide order information to the cooks. Remote order displays are often used in conjunction with UnifiedPOS bump bars. The bump bars are used to bump the order off the display when it is finished and delivered to customers. Properly managing the creation and delivery of customer orders requires a clock to be assigned to each order. These displays are quite powerful and can display graphics, colors, and text. They can be divided into regions so each order can be in its own area of the screen and individually updated. They can also have touchscreens and integrated bump bar capability for moving orders around and off the screen. They can also support different character sets in order to be used in different countries.

- *RFID scanner*—RFID (radio frequency ID) arrived on the scene several years ago and held great promise to solve the accurate inventory and loss-prevention problem. Unfortunately, people who didn't understand the science greatly overplayed the privacy issues, thus reducing the promising return for this technology. However, RFID tags have found a home in the supply chain and warehouse areas. Where retailers and vendors are able to improve the effectiveness of tracking and accounting for inventory. To support this, ARTS standardized the interface for reading and writing to these RFID tags under UnifiedPOS.

- *scale*—the scale is used to measure and communicate the weight or, more correctly, the mass of an object to a POS. Not only does it provide the weight, but it can also calculate the price of the items being weighed. This could be used in a deli environment where customers order a pound of ham; the scale can weigh it and create a label to be put on the package. In a more advanced environment, the label can be a UPC code that the POS reads and goes to the scale to automatically enter the correct weight and price.

- *scanner*—the scanner device reads encoded data from a label.

- *signature capture*—the signature device basically returns a set of (X, Y) coordinates representing customer signatures. The origin is the upper left corner at (0,0) with the lower right being (maximum X, maximum Y). The granularity of the device is defined by the resolution of the pixels. The device is able to display a form for customers to enter signatures with a way for customers to indicate that they are finished.

- *smart card reader*—a smart card is a credit-card-sized card that contains an embedded integrated circuit chip. Because of the presence of this chip, a variety of information can be stored locally on the card. These cards can store a person's financial balance to allow for offline authorization of purchases and/or identification information to validate the individual using the card. They are used like a credit card to purchase items, but they are much more secure. The embedded chip does require a different kind of reader. UnifiedPOS calls the reader a smart card reader/writer (SCR/W). There are two types of readers; one is contactless where customers only wave their cards next to the device. The other is a contact type similar to a traditional mag stripe reader. The SCR/W must be able to read a variety of different formats from simple memory cards to cards with segmented memory (for security) and stored value cards. This device has been widely adopted in Japan and the European Union. Because of its security capability, it will eventually replace all credit cards.

- *tone indicator*—the tone indicator is a device that emanates a sound under programmatic control. It is typically used anytime a signal is necessary to operate the POS. For example, it might be used to signal that a car has entered the drive-thru lane or a customer's order is ready for pickup.

Section 8.7.3.2: Signature Capture and Online-Offline Debit RFP

This is the only hardware-oriented RFP in the collection. It is written to enable retailers to purchase a signature capture device. It includes functionality around security, data management, and disaster recovery.

The functions covered under this RFP start with identifying which ARTS standards the device is compliant with. It then goes on to the display, the device environment, the device physical attributes, software development and configuration, corporate systems hardware/software, and security.

Section 8.7.4: The Customer Engine (Customer)

Customers are the reason retailers are in business. The customer engine is where all customer information is implemented in the POS and is used to tie loyalty accounts with a particular transaction. If a customer is using points to pay for an item or is collecting points with a purchase, the customer engine looks up the customer.

The entry of a customer's loyalty account can be done at any time during the transaction. While the cashier is busy scanning the items, the loyalty system can look up the customer and determine if he or she qualifies for any rewards or discounts. When the transaction is complete, the POS can send the shopping basket to the loyalty system so customers can get credit for their purchases.

Section 8.7.4.1: Price/Customer Interface

Price engines are used to calculate the prices of shopping baskets. Bringing in customer information makes the complexity of the price engine go up significantly. You have to find the best price for a shopping basket, and you need to take into account the potential to purchase the item with loyalty points, getting a price reduction for being a loyal customer, or taking advantage of a targeted offer.

Section 8.8: How Do I Buy a POS? (POS Software RFP)

ARTS POS RFP V2.0.0

In 2003, ARTS was asked to help retailers purchase new equipment and applications by writing requests for proposals or invitations to tender. The first RFP published by ARTS was for purchasing a POS. These RFPs are full of features and functions.

In 2007, version two was published. The POS RFP has over fifteen tabs with hundreds of features. The POS RFP covers all the various engines (item, price, tax, tender, etc.) that a POS needs to operate. Some of the tabs are a set of features targeted at a specific segment. For example, there is a tab for forecourt (gas) and another tab for food service. When the POS RFP was released, the first company to use it got an RFP for a new POS on the street in twelve man-days. They estimated it saved them over $100,000.

Another CIO pointed out that even that cost was less than the cost of setting up the first meeting to begin putting together an RFP. These RFPs are very cost-effective documents.

The POS RFP is divided by functions. The functions are sales transactions, miscellaneous transactions, multichannel sales, receipts, tendering, taxation, cash management, item-price maintenance, manager-specific functions, worker-specific functions, training, marketing (loyalty), reports, store operations, loss prevention, and system events.

One of the most important components of all the RFPs is the glossary. These terms and definitions set a standard for the meanings within the RFP. This way, retailers and vendors who respond will speak the same language. The ultimate goals are to level the playing field, have equal understanding, and compare all responses equally. These are also significant in ARTS since they help standardized terms across ARTS's products.

Section 8.9: Change 4 Charity

ARTS XML Change 4 Charity
Technical Specification V1.0.0

For years, there has been a jar at the checkout stand for customers to donate change to a particular charity. Every Christmas, bell ringers stand outside in the cold to collect change for their charities. When people started paying their transactions with debit cards, there was less change to put in the jars.

The ARTS Change 4 Charity XML standard allows customers to donate to one or more charities during the checkout-tendering process. The amount goes to a charity processor who funnels the donation to the appropriate charity.

CHAPTER 9

ARTS SOA Interface Support

To support the SOA model, ARTS is SOA enabling its XML schemas, such as the Transaction Tax, Customer, Traceability, Item Maintenance, Price, Inventory Management, Stored Value, Time Punches, Product Content Management, ARTS Interface for Donations, Location, and Compliance Audit Interchange by creating a set of service XML schemas.

Section 9.1: Retail Transaction Interface

ARTS XML Retail Transaction Interface Technical Specification V1.0.0

For retailers wishing to take advantage of SOA and cloud computing, ARTS created the Retail Transaction Interface (RTI) XML Standard to separate the POSLog into its constituent components to allow for service-oriented choreography. It can be used to implement multiple-user touch points, such as kiosks, self-checkout, handhelds, mobile, or websites

RTI only deals with selling; therefore, RTI is the selected subset of POSLog that deals with selling, i.e., a customer-order transaction. It is built following the ARTS SOA Best Practices white paper, and as such, it defines a set of seventeen service operations that deal with this sales process.

RTI is a higher-level composite service that begins with a "transaction begin" and finishes with a "transaction finished." Between the two end points, it allows for the addition, cancellation, updating of items, customers, coupons, tenders, etc. Basically, it provides all the steps in the creation of a retail transaction as individual services.

The beauty of SOA is the ability to choreograph these services in a wide variety of ways to solve different business processes. With RTI, retailers can create a process to manage layaways or one to manage customer service, as well as traditional POS.

Section 9.2: Self-Service Order Interface (SSOI)

ARTS XML Self-Service Order Interface
Technical Specification V1.0.0

Figure 36: SSOI

Self-service order interface is an implementation of RTI for handling online ordering. It is used primarily in the food-service industry, where it allows customers to order from a store in real time.

Customers can place orders, give arrival information, and pay with their credit cards using a website or mobile application before they arrive at the store. This allows them to skip the ordering line when arriving at the store to pick up their orders and go directly to the pickup line. This reduces their wait time and efficiently uses the store associates' time.

Customers don't have to wait in line to order and then wait for their food to be prepared, resulting in happier customers. Retailers can more efficiently schedule the food preparation in their kitchens, which means better optimization of staff, which means more customers can be served. This results in more income for retailers.

By having a conversation with customers through the SSOI interface, retailers can help customers with their purchases. For example, if a desired item is out of stock, retailers can inform their customers and suggest alternatives. With cross-selling or upselling, retailers may inform customers about a particular wine that would go well with a selection.

If something happens on the way to the store and the retailers run out of stock, customers can be contacted so that alternatives can be suggested. If customers have loyalty accounts, retailers can save their orders. If customers have certain food or preparation preferences, retailers are aware of them in advance. This reduces the time it takes to place the order and eliminates mistakes associated with the normal order process. They are like individual menus built by previous orders, providing the ultimate customer experience.

CHAPTER 10

Make a Profit

Figure 37: Make a Profit

Making a profit is the reason most businesses exist! Without making a profit, there is fundamentally no way retailers can stay in business. But how does one know? Business analytics are used to measure the information contained primarily in the sales information, but they take many other pieces of data into account. With this information, a set of key performance indicators (KPI) is created. These numbers can help the people in charge understand what is selling and how they are doing financially.

There are several pieces involved in figuring out if there is a profit. The first piece is called reconciliation. Reconciliation takes the money in the individual tills and matches it against the total sales for the till. This is used to verify that the operator is honest and tells exactly how much in total sales occurred. Reconciliation results are reported and stored as an ARTS POSLog Control Transaction. Loss prevention is another piece in helping figure out what it takes to make a profit and helps figure out if things are being taken.

The next discussion is around POS events. These events are sent typically to the store manager to keep them informed of actions around the POS. It helps them understand who is on a particular POS, and what is happening without standing around and watching.

One of the other keys to profitability is inventory management. In a small store, such as a quick-service restaurant or a convenience store, there will be a limited number of POS systems. To leverage this equipment, POSLog allows one to record inventory transactions. It can record inbound and outbound inventory movement.

Now that all this information is available, the discussion turns to how to analyze store operations. ARTS provides a set of KPIs and a data warehouse to help analyze how a particular store is doing. In order to purchase a business intelligence solution, ARTS provides a Business Intelligence RFP to help retailers purchase a business intelligence application.

In addition to understanding the numbers, the people in charge need to monitor losses. To help with this, ARTS created a loss-prevention RFP.

Finally, it discusses the largest controllable expense retailers have: the associates. ARTS has support in two areas; the first is understanding the capabilities and availabilities of the workforce to make sure they have the right person with the right skills on a particular job. The second area of support is recording time and attendance time punches. These can come from time clocks or from POS, especially when the POS can lock and unlock to allow the operator to secure the POS while helping customers.

Section 10.1: Financial Reconciliation

A tender control transaction reports non-transactional financial data. It supports controlling the internal movement of money and is the non-transactional tender component of POSLog. It covers tender actions that can be performed at the POS and in the cash office (tender float, loans, pickups, pay-ins, disbursements, safe drops, etc.).

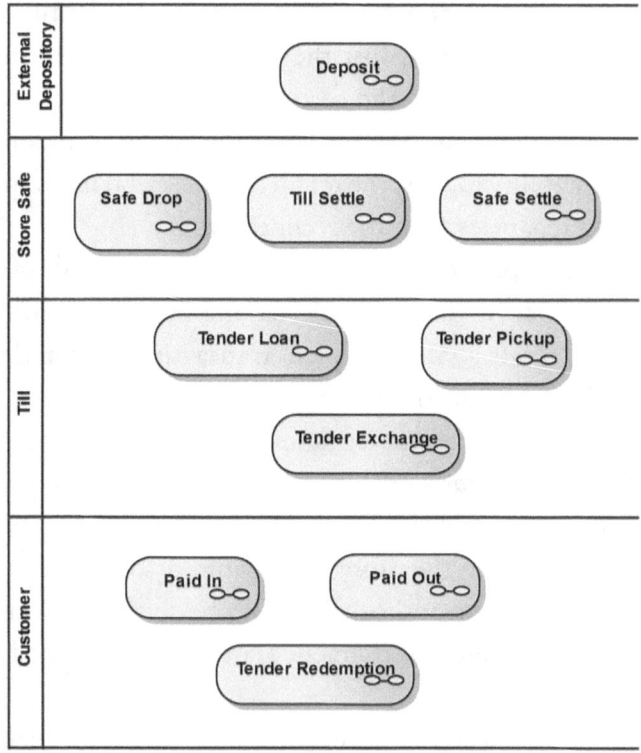

Figure 38: Tender Settlement Options

- *deposit*—reports when money is taken out of the store and put on deposit at the bank.
- *safe drop*—reports when money is taken from the till and put in a safe. Typically used in a convenience store where the safe is in the floor under the POS. Today there are tills that can make an

automatic safe drop when a drawer limit is reached in the till. This is great for the safety of the store associates.

- *till settle*—in UnifiedPOS, an event is generated every time a till (cash drawer insert) is put in or taken out of the cash drawer at the POS. Every day at the end of the operator's shift, these tills get settled. The money in each till is counted and sorted by tender type (cash, credit, check) and denomination. The money is then stored (typically) in the store safe. Periodically, it gets picked up and deposited in the bank. The till settlement is then reconciled against the transactional sales information. The goal is to have the settlement detail exactly match the transaction detail. Since POSs are operated in one of two accountability modes, the retailer defines who has responsibility for discrepancies with the reconciliation.

- *safe settle*—periodically, the personnel in the cash office count all the cash in the store safe (at the beginning and end of a shift) to create a safe settlement transaction. When the amount in the cash office goes over a predefined level, a bank deposit is generated, and the money is transferred to the bank.

- *external depository settlement transaction*—it is possible for money to be temporarily stored in other places besides the cash drawer or the store safe while associates take breaks. These external depositories have to be settled periodically. An external depository settlement transaction is created to report the settlement.

- *tender loan*—when a cashier runs short of change during a shift, money is loaned to him or her from the cash office.

- *tender pickup*—when a drawer limit is reached, money is taken from the till and put in the cash office.

- *tender exchange*—this is similar to a tender loan, but the money comes from another POS. When reconciliation is done, both tills must account for the exchange.

- *paid in*—money is paid to retailers from a source that is not part of a retail transaction. For example, a hot dog vendor might pay for the right to sell the hot dogs.
- *paid out*—money is taken out of the till to pay vendors. For example, this is a way to pay a window washer.
- *tender redemption*—the customer has a voucher. In some cases, he or she is allowed to exchange this voucher for cash.

Section 10.1.1: Payment Reconciliation

To make things more complicated, the banks and payment acquirers reconcile on different schedules than retailers do. Most normal stores that open in the morning and close in the evening don't really have a problem since the payment companies will settle sometime during the night, which corresponds with the reconciliation process for retailers.

However, in twenty-four-hour stores, this is a problem. Typically twenty-four-hour operations close their store sometime in the middle of the night for one minute and reopen immediately. The first problem occurs if they are in the process of checking out customers at this close time because that transaction started on one business day and finished on a different business day. This isn't normally a problem since these retailers try not to close a POS in the middle of a transaction. The important time is when the transaction is tendered, not when the items are scanned in.

The real problem occurs if the time when the acquirer who manages credit- and debit-card authorizations reconciles their books is different from when the POS is reconciled. For example, if the acquirer closes the books at midnight, but the retailer doesn't close the books for two hours, how do you reconcile the sales between midnight and two? The sales show up on the POS between midnight and two, but the debit/credit doesn't show up till the next day.

On the other side, yesterday's finances show up on today's reconciliation, but the items sold were on yesterday's reconciliation.

Section 10.2: POS Events (Control Transaction)

A control transaction can be thought of as an event. Its primary purpose is to feed in-store systems such as loss prevention or store operations with real-time information. Being an event enables quicker responses to issues as soon as they arise.

It encompasses all administrative and control actions that can be performed at the POS (sign-on, sign-off, lock workstation, unlock workstation, open cash drawer, session or shift close, etc.).

Section 10.2.1: Till Movement

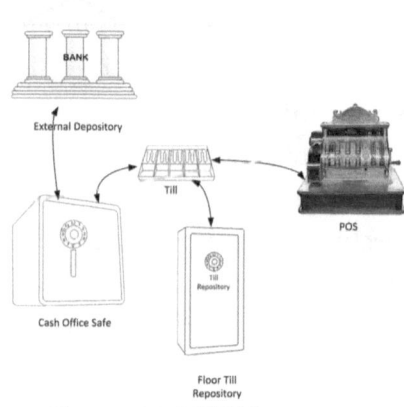

Figure 39: Till Movement

The till is the insert that goes into the cash drawer. In the cashier-accountability mode, the cashier is responsible for all the cash and related transactions from the time the cashier checks the till out from the cash office until he or she checks it back in. At that point, reconciliation is done to balance the till against all the transactions. The ARTS Data Model tracks the period, amounts, workstations, operators, and any till movements during that period.

Till movement can occur when an operator goes on break and puts the till in a temporary repository. When the operator returns from break, he or she retrieves the till and is assigned to a different POS to continue working. The complication comes from reconciling working at different workstations for different periods during one shift.

Tracking the movement of the till is important from a loss-prevention perspective. To support this, the ARTS Data Model records the till movement and has a till report under store operations.

Section 10.2.2: Store Operations Timing

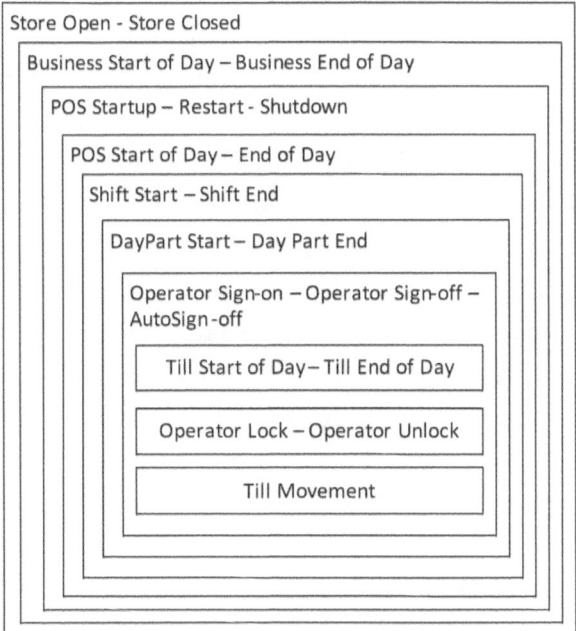

Figure 40: Transaction Context

Throughout the enterprise, there is a need to know the current state of the stores, associates, tills, day parts, and the context of when a transaction took place. POSLog reports these changes as control transactions.

Many retailers allow associates into the stores before customers are allowed in. They use this time to prepare the stores for the day's sales. The same thing happens at the other end of the day; they close the store before the associates go home. While the store is closed, shelves get restocked, and floors are swept.

Most businesses operate on a business day that starts in the morning when customers are allowed in and closes in the evening when the last customer leaves. For accounting purposes, each business day is a financial reporting period. A profit-and-loss statement can be generated. This is a traditional model. The reason is tied to technology.

Before computers, the person in charge (owner, manager, etc.) would balance the books at the end of the day by counting the money in the till and comparing it against the receipt tape. The money would be sent to the bank for safekeeping. When credit cards came into being, there needed to be a time when the credit card company could do the same thing. At this point, the credit card companies could balance their books and transfer money from customers to retailers.

On the operational side, inventory could be analyzed and appropriate restocking could take place. Other operations, such as loss-prevention analysis (comparing actual sales against inventory counts), could occur.

Twenty-four-hour stores mixed up this model because there was no definitive time when those store operations could occur. With the arrival of the Internet, the operations became really blurred. Fully supporting customers and keeping them satisfied required real-time inventory reservations. Even in twenty-four-hour operations, the books had to be closed and money transferred at the end of a period. Normally this business day occurs on a twenty-four-hour period, but sometimes—typically in the Christmas season—the business day could encompass multiple physical days.

When the store is open, one must start the various workstations. Not all workstations are normally started at the start of the business day, but ARTS has the ability to report when each workstation is started, shut down, or rebooted. The next level of reporting occurs when a workstation starts operations at the start of day.

Once the workstation is up and ready to start selling, the next set of control transactions occurs in a dynamic fashion. For example, retailers may require an operator to sign in at their workstation to start the shift before putting the till insert into the cash drawer. Or they may already have a till inserted in the cash drawer, and the operator simply needs to sign in to start selling.

If retailers are using a UnifiedPOS Cash Drawer and Till combination, the insertion of the till causes an event. The event can generate a till start-of-day control transaction to track the movement of the till throughout the day. In operator-accountability mode, retailers want to track the insertion and removal of the till in conjunction with the transactions that occurred while the till was in the workstation.

When operators take breaks, they can remove the till, put it in a till repository, and go on break. When they return from their breaks, they pick up their tills and may go to different workstations. Reconciling this can involve transactions entered at different workstations throughout the day. At the end of their shifts, they remove the tills and take them to the cash office for counting and sending to the external repository (the bank).

Another way to track an operator is have him or her signing into the workstation before starting work. As operators move around the store during their shifts, they can sign in/out at different POSs. That control transaction can be used in the reconciliation process. In addition, signing in and out is an automatic sign-out. If operators leave their workstations, the workstations can automatically sign out the operator.

On the other hand, if operators intentionally leave their workstations to help customers or stock shelves, they can lock their workstations and help customers. When they return, they can unlock the workstations to continue operations. By their very natures, the last few logging operations can be asynchronous, occurring in any order.

In operator-accountability mode, every transaction that operators ring will be assigned to them. At the end of their shifts, they will log off the POS. A settlement transaction is attached to this logoff transaction, sent to the back office in a POSLog Control Transaction, and used in the reconciliation process.

In register-accountability mode, multiple operators ring transactions on a single terminal during a single session. An operator uses his or her own operator ID to track the individual transactions during each session. At the end of the session, a POSLog Control Transaction reports the settlement information to the back office for reconciliation.

Section 10.2.2.1: Day Part Scheduling

In the food-service industry, sales are tracked throughout the day by a "day part." A day part is typically breakfast, lunch, or dinner. Most companies operate with shifts that occur at the same time every day:

day, swing and graveyard. Shifts and day parts are independent of each other. An associate can come to work at a food-service establishment in the middle of the breakfast day part and leave in the middle of the lunch day part. If the company designates it, then this shift can be a "day" shift.

Section 10.2.3: Miscellaneous Control Transactions

Here is a sampling of additional POSLog Control Transactions:

- If the operator changes his or her password, a "password change control transaction" is sent to record this event.
- If the operator opens the till outside of a normal transaction, a "no-sale transaction" occurs, and there is the potential for someone to take money out of the till. A no-sale control transaction is generated and stored in the ARTS Data Model.
- A post void occurs immediately after a retail transaction is complete. It comes from the olden days when the transaction was stored in memory and had not yet been written to the ARTS Data Model. In this case, the post void removed the transaction from memory.
- When a transaction changes state, a POSLog Control Transaction is generated.
- When too much money is in the till, a drawer limit alert is generated and reported in a POSLog Control Transaction. This informs the store manager that there is too much money in the till for safety and that a tender pickup should occur. When it does, this is reported as a POSLog Tender Control Transaction. Most POS systems allow this limit to be configured by the store management.

Section 10.3: Inventory Control Transaction

A POSLog Inventory Control Transaction allows smaller retailers to leverage the hardware in the store to perform multiple different functions; an example is reporting inventory status. The inventory control component of POSLog allows the use of the POS as an interface to the inventory system for recording information such as goods received notices (GRN), inventory counts, and return to vendor (RTV).

Section 10.3.1: Vendor Management

A vendor is an entity (person or company) that sells goods and/or services to an enterprise or retail store. This is a generalization of entities like supplier, carrier, contractor, etc. It encompasses companies that sell anything of a commercial nature from hardware or software to carpenters. It can encompass retailers, such as sidewalk vendors who sell hot dogs. Lease departments are also a type of vendor. For example, the leased jewelry department is a type of vendor.

There are also vendors who sell to businesses. Because this is such a heavily overloaded term that can relate to either side of retailers, there can be much confusion over the intent of the term. A generic definition might be a company that promotes or exchanges goods or services for money to retailers. This definition can include distributors, wholesalers, merchants, and agents. Fundamentally, it is about managing relationships on the business-to-business side.

Some film vendors distribute their movies through distributors that sell the movies to retailers. The vendor from which the retailers purchase these movies is the distributor, and there are different vendors who manufacture (promote) the movie.

In the fuel world, the store purchases fuel from the jobber (also called a distributor or a vendor). The jobber receives fuel from the manufacturer and delivers to the store. Through credit card purchases, the store pays the manufacturer. The manufacturer pays the jobber.

A company in the food-service industry (Braums) controls everything from the farm to customers. The company is involved in the work normally performed by suppliers to grow cattle all the way to providing the hamburgers for their stores. In the end, we have a retailer who is also a vendor. This business model muddies the water between vendors and retailers.

ARTS Data Model supports contact information about vendors. A more detailed set of information is contained in the vendor sections of the Master Data Management RFP. In the RFP, areas such as contracts and performance evaluation are detailed.

Section 10.4: How Does a Company Know If It Is Doing Fine? The KPI

As the story goes, Sam Walton would carry a notebook around his stores. In this notebook, he kept notes on the things he wanted to track. From these, he would make purchasing decisions. Mr. Walton had figured out what measures he needed to run his business and was quite successful at it.

An old adage says that the things that get measured get done. In retail, this is done with monitoring a set of KPIs that measure various aspects of the business.

Leaders, whether they are leading the company or leading one of the departments, cannot know all the details about every item for which they are responsible. To help sort out what is happening, they use these key performance indicators. What are KPIs? Sometimes they are strategic, and other times, they are simply repeatable goals.

Sometimes the SMART criteria for setting these KPIs are used: specific, measurable, achievable, relevant, and timed. There are potentially hundreds of different ways to measure the performance of a company. The information an executive would need to run an entire company would not necessarily be the same as what a department lead would need. Just like with Mr. Walton, each individual must have a good understanding of what is important for running his or her area and must identify the key performance indicators to support these areas.

ARTS Key Performance Measures Technical Report V3.0.0.

ARTS produced a white paper that defined sets of KPIs around three areas: sales, inventory, and customer (more will be added in the future).

The sales KPIs answer how are sales doing compared to last period. Which stores are selling less or more based on their locations or on sales per square foot?

The inventory KPIs answering whether stores have enough inventory on hand. Do I have the right assortment? Am I making a profit on my inventory (not too much, not too little, just right)? Am I maximizing company resources? If video analytics is brought into the picture, retailers can see what is not selling—and where it is located in the store—and determine if there is any correlation.

The customer KPIs determine who the customers are. How can I make money on them? These are particularly important since a majority of retailers' sales are to known customers. The customer KPIs added an enormous amount of demographic, psychographic, and geographic information to the ARTS Data Model.

ARTS has taken these KPIs and created an ARTS Data Warehouse Snowflake Model that is tightly integrated with the ARTS Operational Data Model.

Section 10.4.1: Business Intelligence (BI) RFP

ARTS Business Intelligence RFP V1.0.0

In 2009, ARTS produced the Business Intelligence RFP to help retailers purchase BI solutions. The goal of the Business Intelligence RFP is to help the enterprise define a business intelligence architecture that provides leaders with the information they need to make timely decisions.

The BI RFP provides information around the list of key performance indicators to help businesses make intelligent decisions for running their companies. Because each company may calculate its KPIs slightly differently, the BI RFP focuses on enumerating and defining these analytics.

The BI RFP takes the KPI and data warehouse discussion and tacks on the remaining components, like a dashboard to offer a complete solution to retailers. There are a lot of components to a good business intelligence solution beyond the KPIs. The RFP covers these areas—database and data warehouse, master data management, ETL (extract, transform, and load) services, and reporting tools.

Besides the normal tabs around describing both retailers and the vendor companies, it contains list of features for how to deliver the BI information. It talks about analytic engines integrating the online analytical processing (OLAP) tool with data-mining tools. Some of the key considerations for business analytics are which dimensions, hierarchies, and metrics are used.

The data warehouse where the information resides needs to be administered and audited. When traffic gets heavy, the solution must be able to balance the load between machines. How does the solution balance this load? The data warehouse architecture is directly related to load balancing. This ties in to how much data transformation is needed to load the data warehouse. This is one of the benefits of using both the tightly coupled ARTS Data Model and ARTS Data Warehouse.

Finally, the whole reason for a business intelligence solution is KPI. The list of KPIs can be used by the individuals running the enterprise to understand how the company is running and what needs to focused on to make the company profitable and keep customers returning.

Section 10.5: POS Loss-Prevention and Exception Reporting RFP

ARTS Loss Prevention (POS Exception Reporting) RFP V1.0.0

In 2004, ARTS produced the Loss Prevention RFP to help retailers purchase loss-prevention applications. The Loss-Prevention RFP covers POS-based exceptions, security and networks, and integration.

The goals of any loss-prevention application are to reduce, shrink, and improve compliance by monitoring the POS. It does this by executing a set of loss-prevention KPIs against various data streams to flag possible fraudulent transactions. They monitor fraudulent transactions and losses that occur from associates doing things wrong or following erroneous procedures.

The loss-prevention application is designed to monitor the POS for behavior that could indicate fraudulent activity. The resultant reduction in shrinkage can enhance the bottom line. Loss prevention covers the POS activity, network security, and user security. One unique aspect of this RFP is the cross-reference between various POS activities and the corresponding support provided by ARTS.

Here is a sample of some of the loss prevention options discussed:

Price Change through Price Overrides:
- These are areas where the price is changed at the POS and have the potential for employee theft.

Speed of Service (items per transaction, orders per operator, velocity by ringing worker, and velocity by item):
- If an employee is running an open till on the drive-thru window after midnight, he or she can be pocketing the transaction money. This can be determined by monitoring the number of items per transaction or how many orders a particular operator has processed as compared to other operators.

165

HR (employee information, commission of abuse by employee):
- Verify that the appropriate associate is on the clock and properly assigned to the job.

Stored Value (how issued, redemption usage):
- Track how associates handle and redeem store value cards

Credit Cards (historical data, credit sales and refunds):
- Perform manual override on a declined credit card.

POSLog—Because POSLog is the heart of retail, it provides the biggest opportunity for retailers to see what is going on in the organization. Here is a sampling of the information one can derive from the POSLog:

- By watching *returns*, one can assess if an associate is giving money back without taking in the item in exchange.
- By watching *cash disbursements*, one can see who is receiving the money and whether retailers are getting a service in exchange (washing windows).
- *Post void* is a void that occurs on the previous transaction. An operator rings up a transaction and then immediately voids it. This provides another opportunity for the operator to be giving money to friends.
- *Over/Shorts* are times when the associate either returns too much money to a friend or takes in too much money from a customer.
- *Price overrides* provide easy times for associates to charge friends less than what the items really cost.
- *No sale* is when the operator opens the cash drawer without scanning any items.

In addition, as discussed elsewhere, ARTS Video Analytics provide another feed into the loss-prevention area.

Section 10.6: Workforce Management

The job of human resources is to make sure retailers have enough people with the right skills at the right times to properly operate the store.

In the human resources world, ARTS concentrates on the parts that are necessary to run a store. Retailers need to be able to schedule associates to cover all work. They need to know the skills of the associates and their availabilities. On the other side, they need to know the tasks that need to be performed and the skills necessary to accomplish those tasks. They need to track what associates worked when and on what jobs. To meet this communication need, ARTS has the Workforce Management RFP, the Worker Management XML Standard, the Time Punch XML Standard, and extensive ARTS Data Model support.

Section 10.6.1: ARTS Workforce Management RFP

ARTS Workforce Management RFP V1.0.0

The Workforce Management RFP deals with defining the capabilities needed in purchasing a workforce management solution. To properly schedule associates, retailers have to account for a number of different criteria. For example, to schedule POS checkout clerks (operators in ARTS), store managers need to have some sort of guidance around estimated sales by hour or by shift. They also need to know who is available with the proper skill sets. They need to know about cleaning and stocking shelves. They need to know when trucks are going to arrive to make sure the right associates are available to unload the trucks and stock the shelves.

On the other side, in order for associates to get paid, they need to be able to track the time punches.

Section 10.6.2: Associate Management

Originally associate management was called worker management, but ARTS decided to adopt a more common term. Over time, expect to see the transition from worker to associate. The term covers anyone who can or will work within the enterprise. For example, contractors are scheduled to clean and polish the floors. This is still a workforce management function—even though the contractor is not an employee.

For the retail operations group, all they care about is the ability to schedule an individual. This means that person has to be available when retailers need him or her, he or she has to have the correct experience, certification, or training to accomplish whatever job the retailers need done. For example, a janitor has a different skill set than a stockperson. On top of that, if associates are dealing with cash, retailers need to make sure they are qualified and reliable. If associates are students, what are their class hours?

On the operational side, they don't need to know personal information, medical insurance, or retirement plans. To that end, ARTS is not a human resources model, but it contains human resources support for assigning the right people to the right positions at the right times.

Section 10.6.3: What Is a Job?

Jobs are discrete pieces of work that may require certain levels of training or certification. Each job has a set of tasks (steps) necessary to accomplish that job. These tasks are associated to a set of data around performing the task, i.e., need a broom to sweep the flop. Certificates and training requirements may be needed to perform certain tasks. Scheduling needs to know how many people can perform the same tasks in one area simultaneously; for example, two associates can restock the shelves in one aisle at the same time.

Section 10.6.4: Access Control—Security

The ARTS Data Model access control view is about the rules for managing access by operators to a variety of retailer resources, such as workstations or applications. When an operator signs in to a workstation, POSLog supports sending a control transaction with a sign-in event to report the operator signed has in to the workstation. The ARTS Data Model creates a history of all these events for review and editing by appropriate individuals. It also tracks tasks to which an associate was assigned and performed.

Section 10.6.5: Workstation Assignment

The retailer needs to keep track of which associate was assigned to which workstation—and when he or she was assigned. In addition, if multiple associates are responsible for a single sale, they may all qualify for a commission. For example, one associate may do a presales pitch, such as showing customers various couches, while a different associate finishes the sale. In addition, retailers needs to track associate discounts to monitor for potential abuse.

Section 10.6.6: Workforce Management XML Standards

In 2004, ARTS produced a set of workforce management schemas. The first was about defining associates and their capabilities. The second was about managing their time punches.

ARTS XML Worker Management Technical Specification V1.0.0

The 101-page Worker Management XML Standard was released on August 12, 2004. There were eleven individuals from ten different companies involved in creating this standard.

An associate is an individual who performs work for a retail location. This individual can be an employee, a contractor, or a temporary associate. The standard provides sending contact information, associate availability, associate status, and associate skill sets and/or certifications. All this is necessary to make sure the proper people are doing the jobs they are capable of doing.

ARTS XML Time Punch Technical Specification V1.0.0

The forty-two-page Time Punch Standard was released on September 8, 2004. There were nine individuals from eight different companies involved in creating this standard.

ARTS's mandate is to not create a schema where one already exists. Several times, ARTS cut this close. Time punch is one of those times. There exists a standards organization called HR-XML that provides a full range of XML standards dealing with HR. Most of these areas, such as insurance coverage, are out of scope for ARTS since ARTS focuses on the operational side of retail.

However, ARTS needed to be able to report time punches from the POS. With this information, retailers can better optimize store operations, a piece of which is having the right people on the right jobs at the right times.

ARTS didn't create these HR schemas in a vacuum. ARTS worked closely with HR-XML to properly create the schemas to support the work of HR-XML, the ARTS Data Model, ARTS XML Common Data, and ARTS XML Best Practices. This is a common practice when ARTS bumps against another standards organization.

As associates clock in and out at various workstations around the retail store or at the POS, they need to report where they are and what they are doing. The ARTS Time Punch XML Standard posts this information to the ARTS Data Model.

Associates sometimes make mistakes; they fail to punch in or punch out. They enter the wrong tasks or fail to enter any tasks. Managers need to be able to fix these mistakes. The ARTS Time Punch XML Standard supports sending corrections to an HR system and/or to the ARTS Data Model Worker Time Punch View.

Since ARTS is not a HR standards body, the ARTS time punches are not targeted to be sent to payroll. Instead they are attended for store operations to make sure the tasks are covered with associates who have the right skills.

Section 10.6.6.1: Labor Schedule

Merriam-Webster defines a schedule as "a procedural plan that indicates the time and sequence of each operation." For retailers, a labor schedule is a plan that describes how a retail location will ensure that it is adequately staffed to meet customer demand and accomplish any ancillary tasks needed to meet customer-service goals or business objectives. This covers everything from taking out the trash to stocking the shelves to helping customers.

To plan the schedule, one first needs to know how much working is forecasted to be done throughout the week. From there, identify the tasks that need to be done. Those tasks have a set of requirements necessary to accomplish those tasks. They need to be organized into jobs that can be done during an associate's shift. A shift indicates when and at what location an associate will work. Shifts may also include rest periods (i.e., paid and unpaid meals and breaks), job assignments, department assignments, and task assignments, while a labor schedule is made up of shifts and may be presented in a number of different ways. For example, it may be presented as a schedule for a specific retail location (e.g., store or department).

To schedule associates, one must know several pieces of information. For example, at the minimum, their availability must be known, what skills they have, and where they live.

CHAPTER 11

Global Retailing

Section 11.1: Factory Audits

ARTS Compliance Audit Interchange
Technical Report V1.0.0

According to Fair Factories Clearinghouse, there are over five thousand factories in the United States. Another report said there are over three hundred thousand factories in the United States. Worldwide, there are an enormous number. Retailers are aware of the need to avoid purchasing products from "substandard" factories or factories that exploit their associates in some manner.

To verify they are buying products from proper factories, auditing programs have come into existence. This generated the need for a large number of auditors. That resulted in a number of auditing companies. Several of these companies joined coalitions to help share their audits and auditing duties. However, there is no central registry to manage all the hundreds of thousands of factories in the world. There's no central numbering scheme to be able to consistently and uniquely identify a factory. In addition, the audits that do exist as being shared use 1990s technology, faxes, mail, etc. Auditing is expensive. On top of that, factories have figured out how to beat the system. If they have a problem and fail an audit, they simply change their name. With no central numbering system and no central registry, factories can exploit their people with little repercussions.

ARTS was brought in as an independent standards body to help create a standard audit format. This will facilitate the sharing of audits electronically. The second part is the creation of a central registry to allow retailers to know what audits have been done in factories they are interested in.

It is quite common for a factory to build products for multiple retailers. Finding out which retailers are having their products built in the same factory was one of the reasons these collaborative efforts came into being. This is the beauty of having one central registry with unique factory numbers. Retailers can find out who else is in the same factory—and whether someone else had an audit already performed on this factory. And it is hard for the factory to hide a bad audit. Now it is possible for almost everybody to win. The associates get to work in safe environments, retailers can verify factory conditions, and customers know the products they are purchasing are coming from a place where exploitation does not occur.

CHAPTER 12

ARTS Data Model Reports

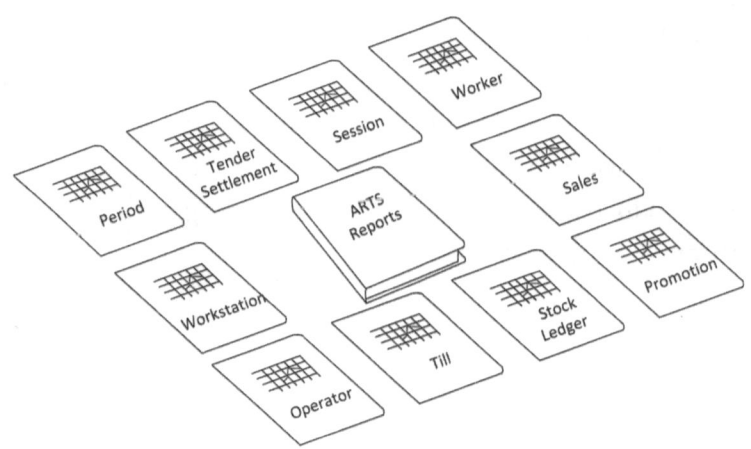

Figure 41: ARTS Data Model Reports

The ARTS data warehouse is a relatively new product. Prior to it, ARTS created a number of reports. Those reports provided useful information and insight into retail operations. The data warehouse doesn't replicate the information contained within these reports.

These reports can be used by loss prevention for verification that all the tender is accounted for. Workforce management can use it to evaluate operator performance. They can also be used to help with proper scheduling. Merchandising can use them to help manage replenishment. Accounting can use them as a part of calculating profit and loss.

Reporting—Store Operations—Tender Settlement

Tender starts at the store safe and is moved to the till to seed the till operations. As items are sold throughout the day, tender is put into the till. When operators take a break, the tills can be temporarily moved to a tender repository (basically a type of safe) on the floor. When the operators come back from the break, they can take the till from the tender repository and put it into their assigned POS to continue selling operations. At the end of their shifts, the operators return the till to the cash office for counting and reconciliation. The tender is then sent to an external depository (the bank).

Throughout this process, the tender is counted and balanced. The reporting of these various settlements is performed through a combination of POSLog Control Transactions and POSLog Tender Control Transactions.

Reporting—Store Operations—Period View

Enterprises are run with a wide variety of time periods. They run the gamut from the various financial periods to a 4-4-5 accounting model (4 quarters, each quarter has 13 weeks grouped into two 4-week "months" and one 5-week "month") to the work periods all the associates work. People get paid, bills get paid, and doors get opened. A variety is reported with a POSLog Control Transaction. Part of the importance is tying all the various histories together from workstation to tender to tax to operators to the store and everything in between.

Reporting—Store Operations—Workstation View

The totals by the workstation are based on the various periods or by settlement. In an operator-accountability mode with a floating till, there are unique periods for which each operator has responsibility that can be matched against the sales for the appropriate period. In register-accountability mode, there are multiple operators for each period with a single till.

The reports include sales count and monetary totals, returns count and monetary totals, or count and percentage of items keyed versus scanned.

Reporting—Store Operations—Session View

The store operations session view gives the totals for each operator by their work periods or by settlement by session. It can also be reported by operator by till. Till-based totals are interesting in a floating till environment. The settlement matches the money in the till with totals from several workstations over different periods.

CHAPTER 13

Unique Components of Food Service

It is said that food service is different from retail, or convenience is different from food service. In reality, most (around 99 percent) of the data is the same for food service, convenience, and retail. Fundamentally, they all sell items. They all have inventory. They all have customers.

When one talks about a hypermarket, all three are sold at the same store under the umbrella of retail. Food service does have some unique aspects; they have kitchens. Convenience has some unique aspects; they sell fuel. Those unique aspects are supported in both the XML schemas and in the ARTS Data Model. Other unique aspects include the tables for customers. A collection of customers in food service is called a party. Food service tracks the size of the party. In ARTS, a party is an abstract base class where different types of parties are derived. For example, a customer is a type of party, but so are suppliers and workers.

Most of ARTS standards are created by subject matter experts coming together under the ARTS umbrella. These individuals take their expertise and merge it with the models that already exist in ARTS to develop new standards. It is possible to seed these work teams with existing intellectual property. A company the author worked for turned over its Speed of Service XML Schema to ARTS to create a standard around this domain.

One of the key components in the quick-serve restaurant world is this speed of service. Any inefficiency in store operations can impact the time it takes to service customers and the number of customers that move through the line in an hour. Before Ray Kroc bought McDonalds, he stood in front of the store and watched the speed with which they moved their customers through the sales process. They had eleven items on the menu, and it took them fifteen seconds to serve each customer.[5] This speed of service was one of the key reasons he bought McDonalds. It is important because there are several measures associated with speed of service. For example, an alert can be generated to alert the store manager if the speed of service exceeds a predefined threshold.

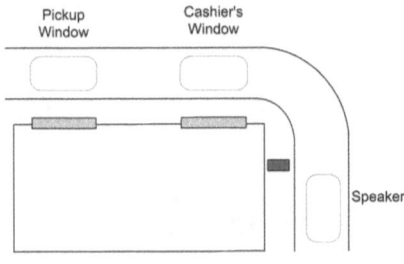

Figure 42: SOS

Food allergies are another concern. This is mostly handled by product labeling. The ARTS Data Model has a view around item description labeling and a table called stock item consumer product label, which carries everything from serving size to hazardous materials.

Section 13.1: Fresh Item Management

ARTS XML FIM Technical Specification V2.0.1

Food safety is another unique concern. Food contamination requires being able to trace the contamination back to its source. No one wants to get sick or wants people to get sick from eating contaminated food. When something happens to perishable items as they move from the farm or factory to the end customer, everyone along the path wants to know as soon as possible so corrective steps can be taken before anyone gets sick. This is challenging since everything that came into contact

---

5   John F. Love, *McDonald's Behind the Arches* (Bantam Trade Paperback).

with the food during its journey from the farm to the table is a potential source of the contamination.

Perishable items are items—produce, meat, batteries, and prescription drugs—that require a controlled environment to maintain quality. Traceability is the ability to track these perishable items back through the food chain to the source, including everything that could impact their quality.

In today's world, perishable items are shipped all over, creating the possibility of a single source spreading contamination over a wide area. Maintaining quality requires the ability to trace back to the origin at each step, every person, and every piece of equipment a perishable item touches all the way back to the farm or the factory that created it. A saw used to cut the steaks might have been used to cut chickens. If the saw was not properly cleaned, there can be cross-contamination from the chickens. If there was a problem with the chickens, that contamination could be transferred to the steaks.

This includes any transformations that occur along the path. For example, chicken salad sandwiches or house salads are made up of a wide variety of items. Each of those items needs to be separately tracked back to the source. A bin of oranges can have items from different lots.

ARTS is responsible for things going on in the retail enterprise, and GS1 is responsible for the business-to-business arena. Together, the two organizations represent the potential for a complete history of the food—all the way back to origination. Because of this clear delineation of responsibilities, ARTS and GS1 worked together to create an ARTS Traceability XML Standard. GS1 tracks the contents from the farm and/or factory to retailers, and ARTS tracks the contents through the retail environment all the way to customers.

This is a little more complicated than it sounds. For example, the supply chain moves things around in boxes, crates, and pallets, and ARTS is about selling individual items. The two different kinds of information (shipping and selling) have to be related in order to track an item all the way back to the farm where it started its journey.

When ARTS takes over as the products reach the dock, two pieces of data come into play. The first is the basic Item ID. But not all things received at the docks can be uniquely identified on customer receipts. For example, a side of beef is eventually carved into many different Item IDs. Until they are turned into saleable items, ARTS tracks them with a lot number. Basically a lot can be broken or subdivided into one or more items. Of course, this is not that simple either. Either of these can be converted into something else. Back to the side of beef: part of it can be ground into hamburger and mixed with tomato paste for spaghetti and meatballs.

Food-service operations are like little factories where fresh items become ingredients in other items like cakes. Traceability must include all the equipment and individuals who are part of this transformation.

Section 13.1.1: Inventory to Transaction Link

In order to track items, the individual items must be bound to key transactions tied to inventory receipt and sales—the two terminal points of retailers' product-handling processes.

On the inventory side, they need to be tied to the appropriate inventory-control document, such as a purchase order, receiving document, advanced ship notice document, transfer document.

To track them on the sale or return transaction side, they are linked to a line item on the retail transaction. If the customers' orders are delivered later, then the fulfillment line item links to the sale and the return line item, thus providing traceability for customer orders. Serialized items link specific instances of items to sell and return line items.

Section 13.1.2: Item Labeling

Item labeling, especially country of origin, is an important requirement mandated by government regulation. These labels come in a variety of shapes and sizes, depending on the item to which they are attached. The content also varies from retailer to retailer and item to item.

The ARTS Data Model supports several of the components of a label, such as carbon footprint, dietary rules, and third-party endorsements. The ARTS Data Model contains the type of label and it stores the human readable descriptions put on the label.

Several entities are used to describe the country of origin, including the basic country of origin for the item and for the supplier. These are based on the standard ISO country codes. With this information, one knows where the item was produced and where the supplier for the item resides. This is important because items can be created in one country but shipped from another.

Knowing where the item was produced is only one piece of the puzzle. Another is the various dates associated with the item. The ARTS Data Model provides a rich set of these dates, such as the production date, packaging date, available-for-sale date, sell-by date, and expiration date. These dates are cross-referenced to the lot number for items that don't have a specific Item ID.

Section 13.1.3: Recall Notification

Now that each item's source is tracked, when an item represents a threat to public safety and health, a recall notice is sent. Individual items covered by that recall can be dealt with. The ARTS Data Model can record the recall event and its instructions to stop selling a particular item. The items or lots identified within the recall are also tracked. These items may be identified directly in the original recall or may be identified by tracing their applications to the recall via traceability: contact with equipment, contact with specific workers, contact with other ingredients, location of items or parent item, and inventory item components. This is necessary to verify compliance with the recall notice.

In the case of lots, the item and its constituent parts are identified to make sure everything is covered. For example, if a recall is done on eggs, any item in which they have been used must also be recalled. Recalls are done on myriad items, but food service is the easiest to understand.

Section 13.2: Kitchen—ProCon—NAFEM

ARTS XML ProCon Technical Specification V1.0.2

The North American Food Equipment Manufacturers Association (NAFEM) standardizes heavy stainless steel food-service equipment like ovens and fryers. As a part of this effort, they created and maintain a standard called the NAFEM Data Protocol (NDP). This protocol is aimed at helping automate kitchens. Basically a kitchen is a mini-factory that builds the items they sell on the premises in real time. NAFEM wanted to take the equipment data and convert it to actionable information for use by applications within the food-service environment by leveraging the synergies of NAFEM and ARTS.

NAFEM Data Protocol brings the equipment communications standard/applications programmers interface (API). ARTS brings the business information through the ARTS XML schemas and the ARTS Data Model. Integrating these two elements enables the necessary environment for the creation of the automated factory. One can convert a recipe into a product by first figuring out what item is needed and then automatically manufacturing that item under control of the recipe. With the enterprise view, it is a natural fit for ARTS to extend its work into the food-service vertical through an interface with the NDP. This automation has the potential to help owners serve more customers with fewer employees while providing consistent products.

Doing this requires an interface that maps the NDP to an ARTS XML schema called Kitchen XML. NAFEM and ARTS came together to create the mapping interface called ProCon (Protocol Converter) to convert the NDP into ARTS XML and convert the ARTS XML back to the NDP protocol.

With this interface, a chicken restaurant can check its sales history (POSLog) and determine that they sell four chickens every day at eleven o'clock. At ten thirty, they can check their inventory (inventory schema) to see how many chickens they have on hand (two). They can see that they need two more chickens. They can go to the recipe application to see what is involved in creating the two additional chickens they need at eleven. The recipe says it takes fifteen minutes to cook a chicken. It feeds this information to the automatic deep fryer, telling the deep fryer that it needs to start frying the chicken at ten forty-five.

CHAPTER 14

Forecourt Unique Components

Over the years, ARTS has worked with many other standards bodies. In the convenience industry, ARTS has worked with PCATS (Petroleum, Convenience Alliance for Technology Standards). Originally PCATS was a branch of the National Association of Convenience Stores, but it was spun off in 2004. In addition, there is an organization in Europe called IFSF (International Forecourt Standards Forum). IFSF is made up of the world's largest petroleum companies.

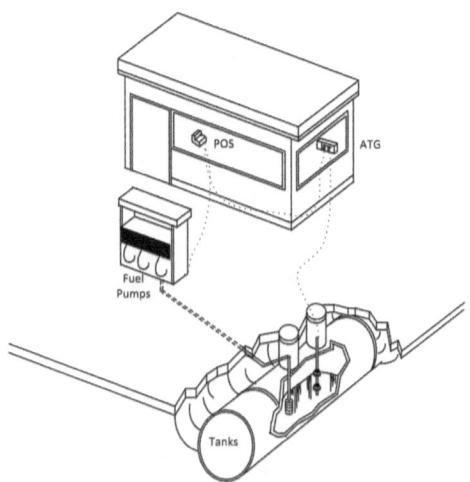

Figure 43: Forecourt Components

The major components of the forecourt start with the POS in the store. The POS is connected to the CRIND (Card Reader in Dispenser) located in the fueling pump. At the end of day, these sales need to be synchronized with the purchases in the stores. The dispenser is connected to the tank (where all kinds of sensors and readings are continuously taking place). Many of these readings are sent to the automatic tank gauging system (ATG) in the store.

Forecourt Fueling Point

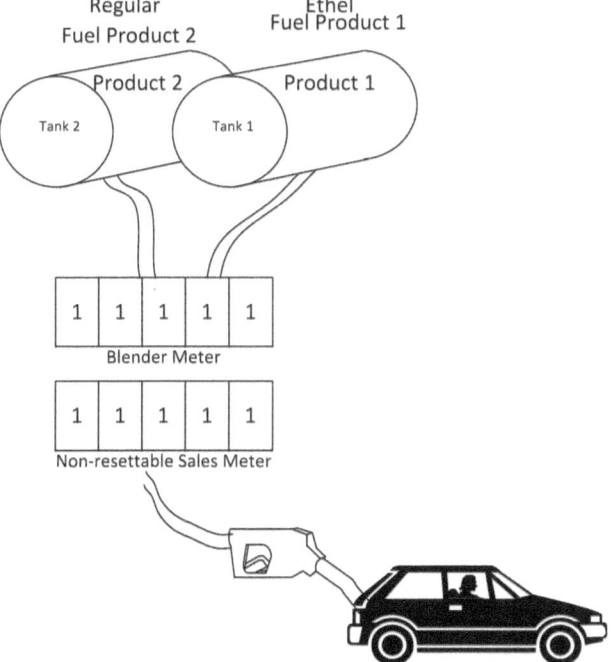

Figure 44: Fueling Point

The dispenser is where gas is pumped into the car. Typically, it has at least two fueling points: one for regular gas and one for high-test gas. The third gas option is generated by a blender that mixes gas from the regular and high-test tanks. The gas is pumped out through a nozzle. When finished pumping, the fuel sale is reported in a fuel sales line item on a retail transaction. The fuel inventory information can be reported through the Item Maintenance XML Standard.

The total amount of fuel is kept by a non-resettable sales meter in the dispenser and summarized by a stock meter and sales meter readings in the ARTS Data Model.

Forecourt Transaction

Traditionally, the tendering of a gas sale from a dispenser in the forecourt was separated from the delivery of the gas into the car. The tendering occurred in the store, and the pumping occurred at the dispenser. Today's modern systems allow both events to occur at the dispenser and eliminates the separation of the actions.

The ARTS Data Model Forecourt View was modeled after the traditional approach, which is still valid in many areas of the world. This led to a couple of problems; in a drive-off, customers would fill the car and drive off without paying. Generally, there were two activities behind this drive-off: customers stole the fuel or simply forgot to pay. In the second case, when they do remember, they come back and correct the oversight. For the correction to occur, the POS in the store has to be able to recall the transaction, add a tender, and close the transaction. This sounds like a normal customer order transaction, and it is.

The unique aspect is that the CRIND is located at the pump, and the transaction is closed in the store. As long as the CRIND can send its transactions to the store POS, this is no different from the deli scenario or any scenario where multiple POS systems are involved in the transaction, such as buying on the web and picking up in the store.

In a pump test performed by a governing agency, a single gallon is pumped into a measured container to validate the accuracy of the pump. Traditionally, the fuel was poured back into the tanks. Today with environmental regulations, tanks are not opened unless a fueling truck is present. The pump test fuel is not returned to the tanks.

In order to correct inventory, a waste transaction is used to account for the loss of fuel.

Forecourt History View

The ARTS Data Model Forecourt History shows the summaries that are needed to reconcile a set of "prepay" and "post pay" with the corresponding fueling transactions that occurred during the current period.

Prepays are used to authorize one or more nozzles to allow fueling to occur. There are two types of prepay. The most common is to preauthorize a specific maximum amount. The fuel is dispensed into the automobile. When finished, the actual amount is charged to consumers. The second method is to charge a minimal amount, such as one dollar. This is to mostly verify the credit/debit card. When the fueling transaction is complete, the correct amount is charged to customers.

The forecourt history reports the sales by nozzle and is settled to verify that the tanks are not leaking, and everything is working correctly.

Forecourt Tank Gauge View

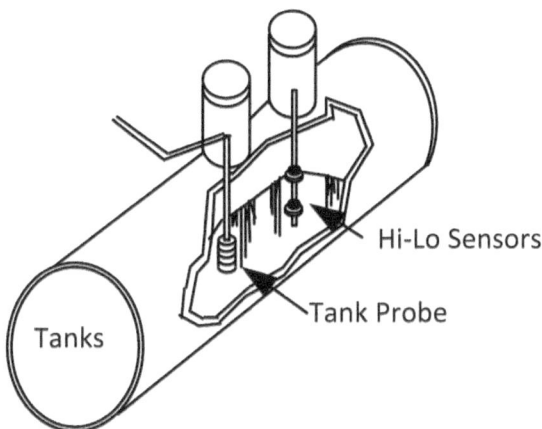

Figure 45: Tank Sensors

Measuring the amount of fuel and water in underground fuel storage tanks traditionally was taken with a stick inserted into the tank. When the stick was removed, the amount of water and fuel was read off the stick. Today, this process has been automated with the use of tank gauges and tank probes. These readings are put into the ARTS Data Model to indicate the fuel inventory. They are used in reconciliation and reordering.

CHAPTER 15

Summary

ARTS has extensive support for nearly all retail activities. This book has attempted to show how all these standards work together to try to get consumers into stores, turn them into customers, and make a profit. There is an enormous amount of supporting details contained in the technical specifications for each standard. UnifiedPOS has over two thousand pages to describe how to use thirty-six devices, basically every kind of device one can attach to a POS anywhere in the world.

There are twenty ARTS XML schemas with thousands of pages of technical documentation. POSLog alone has over five hundred use cases to show how to use it in almost any context. There are thirty subject areas in the ARTS Data Model, including over five thousand attributes and seven hundred entities. There are nine RFPs to help retailers and vendors buy and sell their applications. Finally, there are seven white papers to explain technology concepts from SOA to social media to customer life cycles.

To summarize how they all relate, here is a brief POS example. Other retail applications have similar in-depth support.

When customers arrive at the checkout stand, a motion sensor can detect their presence. When customers put their items on the conveyor belt, the belts can move items forward to be scanned by a scanner or an image scanner. If an RFID tag is attached to the item, then the RFID scanner can identify what kind of item it is. The item and its price can be looked up from the Item and Price Management ARTS Data Model Subject Area and communicated to the POS with the Item Maintenance and Price XML Standards.

The price engine can determine whether any promotions are applicable by evaluating the shopping basket with respect to the Item Price Derivation Data Model View. While the items are being scanned, customers can be kept informed on a line display. Item images can be retrieved using the Product Content Management XML Standard. If the item needs to be weighed, a scale can be used to weigh the item. As the items are entered, any associated taxes can be retrieved from the tax engine with the Transaction Tax XML Standard.

To control access to the POS, a biometric device can be used to read the associate's fingerprint. Or a key lock can be used. A key lock can also allow changing the state of the POS. A lighting device can be turned on and/or made to blink. Once the associate has gained access to the POS, the POS keyboard enables the associate to manually enter customer purchases.

There are a variety of devices for tendering. In the POS for cash, a cash drawer can tell what insert is in this cash drawer. The insert contains the cash and can be retrieved by an associate from a secure location. If a credit or debit card is used, a mag stripe reader can be used to read the card or a credit authorization terminal (CAT) or an electronic value reader/writer is used to authorize the transaction.

A point card is a variation of a credit card where customers point their cards to have them read. The smart card reader is a type of stored value where the amount is stored on the card. If a check is used, a check scanner is used to read the check while MICR is used to read the bank numbers. For security, a PIN pad can be used to have customers enter their PIN number.

The tender entry can be transmitted to the tender engine by using the POSLog XML Standard. When the transaction is complete, customers can sign on the signature capture device. The customer's loyalty number can also be read with these devices and then looked up in the Customer Relationship Management Data Model Subject Area and communicated to the POS with the Customer XML Standard.

If there is a vending machine, a bill acceptor or coin acceptor is necessary to accept money from customers. The bill dispenser or coin dispenser will return change to customers. When put together in one device, it is called a cash changer. The item dispenser can be used to deliver the items to customers.

In a food-service establishment, the kitchen system displays several customers' orders on a remote order system. When the order is delivered, a bump bar is used to remove the item from the remote order display. Whenever a button is pushed, a tone can be sounded from the tone indicator.

To permanently record and store transaction history, the electronic journal or fiscal printer is used. If one wishes to securely keep transaction information in memory, a hard totals device is called for. In addition, the transaction can be communicated to the accounting system using the POSLog XML Standard and recorded into the POSLog Data Model Subject Area. The purchased items can be communicated to and removed from the inventory-management data model subject area with the Inventory XML Standard.

In a self-checkout environment, a gate can allow customers to leave after a transaction is completed. To provide controlled power to all, a POS Power Device is available.

Whew! This is just one application. ARTS has just as extensive support for many systems within the retail environment. Because there are too many details to include here, this book has touched the tip of the iceberg to show everything in context. All of ARTS's products have extensive technical support to explain the subject areas in great detail. If a deep understanding of retail technology is desired, all that is needed is downloading and reading these published artifacts.

For additional details, please go to www.nrf-arts.org and download the appropriate standards for your world. But more importantly, join ARTS and share your knowledge to add more content to the ARTS inventory of products.

CHAPTER 16

ARTS Product Lines

Section 16.1: NRF Papers

NRF Color Guide
NRF Product Attribute System

Section 16.2: White Papers

ARTS Best Practice for Process Modeling V2.0 20110921
ARTS Cloud Computing Technical Report 20091212
ARTS Consumer-Customer Life Cycle Model Technical Report V1 0
    20130503
ARTS XML Domain Modeling Technical Report V1.0.0
ARTS XML Extending Schemas Technical Report V2.1 20101111
ARTS Infrastructure Technical Specification V1.0 20030826
ARTS Coordinate System Insertion Points White Paper V1.0.0 20130924
ARTS Mobile Retailing Blueprint V2.0.0 20110104
ARTS Mobile Integration White Paper Final V2 2012-05-21
ARTS XML Payments Integration White Paper V2 20121011
PCI Best Practices 20090112
SOA Best Practices Technical Report V1.2.0 20081225
ARTS XML SOA Blueprint V1.2.0 20081225

ARTS Social Blueprint 20120105

CR Why Business Process Modeling 2010-11-22

Section 16.3: ARTS Data Model

Operational Data Model V7.0

Data Warehouse V3.0

Section 16.4: XML Schemas

ARTS XML Associate Management Technical Specification V2.0.0 20070917

ARTS XML ARTS Interface for Donations Technical Specification V1.0.0

ARTS IXRetail Comparison Shopping Engine Technical Specification V1.0 20061006

ARTS XML Compliance Audit Interchange Technical Specification 20130724

ARTS XML Customer Technical Specification V3.0.0 20091217

ARTS XML Digital Receipt Technical Specification V2.0 20110706

ARTS XML FIM V2 Technical Specification (Traceability)

ARTS XML Inventory Technical Specification V2.1.0 201112125

ARTS XML Item Maintenance Technical Specification V1.3.0 20111227

ARTS XML ProCon Technical Specification V1 0 20070528 (Kitchen

ARTS XML Location Technical Specification V1.0.0 20130710

ARTS XML NEAR Technical Specification 20060811 Notification Event Architecture for Retail

ARTS XML PCM Technical Specification V3.1.0 20120201

ARTS XML POSLog Technical Specification V6.0.0 20130930

ARTS XML Price Technical Specification V2.0.1 20050601 (Price Service Interface)

ARTS IXRetail Remote Equipment Monitoring and Control Technical Specification V1.0

ARTS XML Retail Transaction Interface Technical Specification V1.0.0 20071225

ARTS XML Self-Service Order Interface Technical Specification V1.0.0 20120419

ARTS XML Stored Value Technical Specification V1.0.020070215

ARTS IXRetail Time Punches Technical Specification V1.0 20040908

ARTS XML Transaction Tax Technical Specification V2.0.0 20081217

ARTS XML Video Analytics Technical Specification V1.0.1 20081007

Section 16.5: UnifiedPOS

UnifiedPOS V1.14 20130901
WamPOS V1.0
WS-POS V1.2
XMLPOS V1.2

Section 16.6: RFPs

POS RFP V2.0 20070403
BI RFP V1 20090415
ARTS Cloud RFP V2.0 9.01.11
Loss Prevention (POS Exception Reporting) RFP 20040625
Master Data Management RFP 20060825
Price Life Cycle Optimization RFP 20051222
Signature Capture Online-Offline Debit RFP 200410
Warehouse Management RFP 20050520
Workforce Management RFP Dec 2007

Section 16.7: Business Process Model

Business Process Model Level 0 and Level 1

BIBLIOGRAPHY

Accounting

Kelley, J. Roland, Jimmy C. McKenzie, and Alton W. Evans. *Business Mathematics*. Boston: Houghton Mifflin Company, 1982.

Kravitz, Wallace W. *Bookkeeping the Easy Way*. Hauppauge: NY Barrons, 1999.

Larson, Kermit D., John J. Wild, and Barbara Chiappetta. *Fundamental Accounting Principles*. New York: McGraw-Hill, 1996.

Pahler, Arnold J., and Joseph E. Mori. *Advanced Accounting: Concepts and Practice*. Orlando: Dryden Press, 2000.

Stanley, Delmar S., and John G. Black. *Practical Accounting*. Pacific Palisades: CA Goodyear, 1976.

Business

Alexander, Bevin. *How Great Generals Win*. New York: Norton, 1993.

Bloom, Martin H. *Business Buying Basics*. San Marcos: CA Robert Erdmann Publishing, 1992.

Dunne, Patrick M., Robert F. Lusch, and David A. Griffith. *Retailing*. Orlando: Harcourt, 2002.

Enrico, Roger, and Jesse Kornbluth. *The Other Guy Blinked: How Pepsi Won the Cola Wars*. New York: Bantam, 1986.

Gates, Bill. *The Road Ahead*. New York: Viking, 1995.

Gill, Michael Gates. *How Starbucks Saved My Life*. New York: Gotham Books, 2008.

Greising, David. *I'd Like the World to Buy a Coke: The Life and Leadership of Roberto Goizueta*. New York: John Wiley and Sons, 1998.

Harvard Business Review on Brand Management. Boston: Harvard Business Review Paperback, 1999.

Kunhardt, Philip B., Jr., Philip B. Kunhardt III, and Peter W. Kunhardt. *P.T. Barnum, America's Greatest Showman*. New York: Alfred A. Knopf, 1995.

Love, John F. *McDonald's: Behind the Arches*. New York: Bantam Trade Paperback, 1995.

MacRae, Norman. *John von Neumann*. New York: Pantheon, 1992.

Marriott, J. W., Jr., and Kathi Ann Brown. *The Spirit to Serve: Marriott's Way*. New York: Harper Perennial, 1997.

McCormack, Mark. *What They Don't Teach You at Harvard Business School*. Toronto: Bantam Books, 1984.

Moritz, Michael. *The Little Kingdom: The Private Story of Apple Computer*. New York: Morrow, 1984.

Newsom, Doug, Judy Vanslyke Turk, and Dean Druckeberg. *This Is PR*. Belmont: NY Wadsworth Publishing Company, 1996.

Risdahl, Aliza Sherman. *The Everything Blogging Book*. Avon: MA Adams Media, 2006.

Trimble, Vance H. *Sam Walton: The Insider Story of America's Richest Man*. New York: Dutton, 1990.

Wallis, Michael. *Oil Man: The Story of Frank Phillips and the Birth of Phillips Petroleum*. New York: Doubleday, 1988.

Walton, Sam, with John Huey. *Sam Walton: Made in America*. New York: Doubleday, 1992.

Watson, Thomas J., Jr., and Peter Petre. *Father, Son, and Co.: My Life at IBM and Beyond*. New York: Bantam, 1990.

White, Richard M., Jr. *The Entrepreneur's Manual*. Radnor: PA Chilton Book Company, 1977.

Business Analytics

Davenport, Thomas H., Jeanne G. Harris, and Robert Morison. *Analytics at Work: Smarter Decisions, Better Results*. Boston: Harvard Business Press, 2010.

Dixit, Avinash, and Barry Nalebuff. *Thinking Strategically*. New York: W. W. Norton and Company, 1991.

Kelley, J. Roland, Jimmy C. McKenzie, and Alton W. Evans. *Business Mathematics*. Houghton Mifflin. Boston, Ma, 1982

Sun-Tzu. *The Art of War*. New York: Barnes and Noble Books, 1994.

Reference

Argenti, Paul A. *The Portable MBA Desk Reference: An Essential Business Companion*. New York: Wiley, 1994.

Glossary of Hospitality Terms. East Lansing: Educational Institute, American Hotel and Motel Association, 1995.

Gookin, Dan, and Wallace Wang. *Illustrated Computer Dictionary for Dummies*. Foster City: CA IDG Books, 1995.

Hissey, Ivan, and Curtis Tappenden. *The Practical Encyclopedia of Cartooning*. London: Lorenz Books, 2009.

Ostrow, Rona, and Sweetman R. Smith. *The Dictionary of Retailing*. New York: Fairchild Book Division, 1985.

Rosenberg, Jerry M. *Dictionary of Business and Management*. New York: Wiley, 1993.

Sippl, Charles J., and Roger J. Sippl. *Computer Dictionary*. Indianapolis: Howard W. Sams and Co., 1983.

The Ultimate Business Dictionary. Cambridge: Perseus Publishing, 2003.

Food Service

Foodservice Sanitation. The Education Foundation of the National Restaurant Association, 1992.

Powers, Tom. *Introduction to Management in the Hospitality Industry.* New York: Wiley, 1992.

Management

Kotter, John P., Leonard A. Schlesinger, and Vijay Sathe. *Organization: Text, Cases and Readings on the Management of Organization Design and Change.* Homewood: IL Irwin, 1986.

Machiavelli, Niccolo. *The Prince.*

Porter, Michael E. *Competitive Advantage: Creating and Sustaining Superior Performance.* New York: Free Press, 1998.

Marketing

Berkowitz, Eric N., Roger A. Kerin, Steven W. Hartley, and William Rudelius. *Marketing 6th Edition.* New York: Irwin McGraw-Hill, 2000.

Dunay, Paul, and Richard Krueger. *Facebook Marketing for Dummies.* Indianapolis: Wiley, 2011.

Meerman, David. *World Wide Rave.* Hoboken: John Wiley and Sons, 2009.

Perreault, William D., Jr., E. Jerome McCarthy. *Basic Marketing: A Global-Managerial Approach.* New York: Irwin McGraw-Hill, 1999.

Ries, Al, and Jack Trout. *Marketing Warfare.* New York: McGraw-Hill, 1986.

Sansevieri, Penny C. *Red Hot Internet Publicity.* Cosimo Books, 2013.

Underhill, Paco. *Why We Buy: The Science of Shopping.* New York: Touchstone, 1999.

White, Sarah, and John Woods. *Do-It-Yourself Advertising*. Holbrook: MA Adams Media Corporation, 1997.

Mobile

Saylor, Michael. *The Mobile Wave*. New York: Vanguard Press, 2012.

Point of Sale

Atkinson, Chuck. *Automation Pays: How to Automate Your Business, Point-of-Sale, and Back Office Management for Retail Stores, Chain Stores, Wholesalers, Mail Order, and Food Service*. Fort Worth: Aces Four Press, 2000.

SOA

Hohpe, Gregor, and Bobby Woolf. *Enterprise Integration Patterns*. Boston: Addison-Wesley, 2004.
Readings in Service Orientation. Microsoft, 2006.

Taxes

Locks, Doris C. *Multistate Sales and Use Tax Manual*. New York: Warren Gorham Lamont, RIA Group, 2000.

Warehouse Management

Tompkins, James A., and Jerry D. Smith. *The Warehouse Management Handbook*. Raleigh: Tompkins Press, 1998.

www.ingramcontent.com/pod-product-compliance
Lightning Source LLC
Chambersburg PA
CBHW030929180526
45163CB00002B/504